DON'T THROW
THE FLAG TOO SOON

To, General Hershey
My friend
Joe Haynes
9/24/15

DON'T THROW
THE FLAG TOO SOON

DR. JOE A. HAYNES
WITH ROBERT WILSON

Pink Kiss Publishing Company
Gautier, Mississippi

Pink Kiss Publishing Company
P.O. Box 744
Gautier, Mississippi 39553
(228) 366-6829
www.pinkkisspublishing.com

Printed in the United States of America.

ISBN 978-0-9895580-5-1

Library of Congress Control Number: 2013918170

Cover designed by Donna Osborn Clark

Interior designed by Glenda A. Wallace

Cover photos by Jay D. Johnson Photography

To Dorothy, Christopher, Kristi, Erriona, Kristion, and all my family and friends.

Acknowledgments

Thanks to my wife, Dorothy, and all of my family for encouraging me to go forward with writing my book.

A special thanks to Mr. Robert Wilson for his advice and assistance in putting this memoir into words.

Thanks to all of my former co-workers, students, teachers, and colleagues that I conferred with to reconstruct much of the information contained in this book.

Special thanks to the Jobs for Mississippi Graduates' (JMG) central office staff for their support over the years.

Thanks to Mr. Art McNally, former director of the National Football League (NFL) officials, for editing much of the information that pertains to the NFL.

Thanks to Mr. Butch Lambert Jr. for his timely advice, for extending his knowledge to me during my early days of officiating in the Southeastern Conference (SEC), and for writing the foreword to this memoir. Butch Lambert Jr. was able to reconstruct what really happened when Nate Anderson and I became the first minority officials in the SEC. The late Butch Lambert Sr. was a role model and supporter all the way.

Thanks to Dr. Robert Fortenberry, my mentor in education and a true humanitarian.

Thanks go out to my legal support team, especially Attorney Shawanesey Howell for her excellent legal advice.

Thanks to my publicist, Shonna Pierce, for her assistance with marketing and promoting.

Thanks to all the persons interviewed for this book (more than sixty-five were interviewed in the process of writing this memoir).

And, finally, thanks to everyone who supported me over the years.

FOREWORD

My long friendship with Joe had its origin in athletics. Joe and I were football-officiating teammates in 1975, working in the top Division I college football league in the nation. I became a Southeastern Conference (SEC) football official in 1974; a year later, Joe joined.

Officials are paid to keep their heads while everyone else loses theirs. Officials must be respectful and listen patiently to coaches, who often have heated emotions, and answer in a matter-of-fact, accommodating, and authoritative manner without losing their cool. Officials must have a presence that exhibits confidence and compassion. Joe has all of these attributes and more.

Joe says that, when he started officiating, he wanted to be an example to young athletes. He hoped he could demonstrate that, by applying oneself in school, as well as athletics, young people would see that hard work could sustain them in all walks of life.

Athletics and education are two fields that can play an integral part in instilling character, integrity, and values in young people. Teachers and coaches have a moral obligation to be a positive influence on those who are seeking, sometimes desperately, clear guidance on those very attributes. Joe has always stressed the importance of knowing how to think things through, of how to make a decision, and most importantly, of being aware of and responsible for the consequences of those decisions.

It's no mistake that Joe ended up in both fields of endeavor: athletics and education. He gives credit, first, to his parents, teachers, coaches, and many other leaders in education and sports.

In addition to these wonderful people, Joe gives my dad, A.C. "Butch" Lambert Sr., credit for mentoring him in his officiating career. My dad, who was the former Mississippi legislator/chairman of the Ways and Means Committee and, later, chairman of the Mississippi State Tax Commission, had retired from his position as an SEC football official in 1981, but he remained an SEC assistant supervisor, both grading and teaching officials, until 1985.

He began mentoring Joe when he became an SEC football official in 1975. Joe was concerned about having to make a close call before 80,000 fans and while the game was being nationally televised. My dad told Joe, as he had told me all my life during his teaching moments, that he wanted the "close call" that decided the game to be on the goal line, because Dad would get the blame, right or wrong. Dad trusted Joe's judgment, and he knew that Joe would be in the right position to make that call. Joe and Dad had many calls that determined the outcome of the game, which fans and coaches did not like, but they were "right!"

Joe and my dad's SEC officiating positions were located on the sidelines and were situated on the line of scrimmage. This meant that all head and assistant coaches were in their ears the entire game. Most times, they were not pleased with whatever had just happened on the field or how the game was going.

My dad, Butch Sr., officiated thirty years in the SEC as a football official, twenty-four years as an SEC basketball official and supervisor, and I officiated twenty-eight years as an SEC football official. When my dad passed away in January 1985 from Lou Gehrig's disease (ALS), Joe was there for me as a colleague and a friend. During our visits, Joe and I would reminisce about my dad and the lessons we had both learned from him that have helped us in life's journey.

In 2006, my dad and I received the Officials Award by the National Football Foundation and College Hall of Fame at their Annual Hall of Fame Induction Ceremony at the Waldorf Astoria Hotel in New York. We were the first father and son to receive that honor. Joe's was one of the first calls I received congratulating us on receiving this very high honor and recognition.

From 1975 to 1983, Joe and I officiated many SEC college football games together. In 1984, Joe, because of his excellent work ethic and his top ratings as an SEC football official year in and year out, was given the opportunity to join the National Football League (NFL), which he accepted. Joe went on to an outstanding career in the NFL, and, when he retired, he became a scout for the NFL, searching for candidates who fulfilled the requirements for NFL football officials.

Certainly, Joe not only fulfilled his goal, but he clearly transcended it. His influence has reached well beyond his imagination. His imprint has clearly been left on young athletes, and they have carried it to everyone they teach and coach. That's how the vision of Joe Haynes has been carried to those who have needed it. That's the imprint of an excellent teacher/educator/coach/official. It is felt and will continue to be through the ages. His grasp, indeed, exceeds his reach.

Don't Throw the Flag Too Soon is a must-read for both younger and older adults no matter what our walk of life, no matter our ethnicity, no matter if we lead or follow, no matter our material possessions, and, certainly, no matter whether we like sports or not. Joe's life is a journey filled with great leaders, role models, mentors, teammates, and friends. As a result of these great people in Joe's life, he has attained these attributes and more, giving him the instincts and the ability to make decisions to give others second chances and redemption.

Joe says, "We condemn people without knowing them! The consequences of giving up on a person and making a final decision without having all the facts can be devastating."

Joe's book shows that, no matter our journey, we should give what we have many times been given — a second chance and a helping hand to our fellow man.

Joe's upbringing and life journey have true meaning for everyone, and I hope you will read and enjoy. Above all, give someone a second chance; don't judge people before you know them, and DON'T THROW THE FLAG TOO SOON!

A.C. "Butch" Lambert Jr.
Southeastern Conference Football Official
1974-2001

~Contents~

PART I

INTRODUCTION

INTRODUCTION

This book is about redemption, second chances, and beating the odds. Amazing things can happen when compassion and thought are mixed with the opportunity for another try. The power of giving extra consideration to things involving the human spirit yields amazing results.

In education and in sports, many opportunities exist that allow us to rethink our decisions before we make a final decision. The consequences of giving up on a person and making a final decision without all of the facts can be devastating.

Oftentimes, within the legal system, we hear about a prosecutor or a legal expert that has rushed to judgment and, for some reason, wants to convict quickly, but, in any situation, we must take into account all of the facts in the case before coming to a decision. *Don't Throw the Flag Too Soon* is all about giving effective thought to a decision from the onset. Many of the decisions that we make in life can be harmful to an individual if the decision is made hastily and without thought. It can have dire consequences that can have a lifelong effect.

As an educator, I like to think positively about the contributions that young people can make when they are given a second chance to use their God-given potential. When our youth are given a second chance, the positive outcomes make up for any time lost in the thought process of decision making.

In sports, we are taught to make good decisions and to make them accurately. The art of making a good decision has the ingredients of thinking it through and giving pause before we decide too quickly and have to defend a decision made in haste. Good judgment is best when all of the ingredients are used on the front end, when it's not too late to do something about the decision.

College and professional athletic teams are coming to grips with the negatives associated with poor decision making that can damage young athletes for a lifetime. Instant replay and not so instant replays were invented to support the objective of getting the call right.

Don't Throw the Flag Too Soon is about taking opportunities to correct poor decisions in a meaningful way — in the game of life or in any setting. When the odds are beaten for not throwing the flag too soon, we rejoice.

Ole Miss football coach, Houston Nutt, one of the most well-respected coaches in the country, made a comment in the fall of 2011 in a story in Jackson, Mississippi's *Clarion-Ledger* about Rebel quarterback, Randall Mackey, who had made the mistake of being in the wrong place at the wrong time. The end result? A decision was made hastily. The coach, in his own words, said that he wished he could reverse his decision.

"I want to make sure that we understand Mackey didn't do anything wrong, except stay out too late. He is not a bad guy or a troublemaker. I wish I had rethought that a little bit."

Mackey was suspended for the season opener against Brigham Young—a game Ole Miss lost.

Much of what is discussed in this book is evidence of not throwing the flag too soon. As a young farm boy, little did I know that the rich determination planted by my parents through tough lessons and tough love would lead to a successful life in education and sports. I was surrounded by exceptional teachers and good people in general that did not throw the flag on me because of any of my shortcomings. They provided praise and support at a critical time in my life. They helped me to set and reach my goals, and they taught me to use my God-given talents. That helped me to begin my life's journey. Some of these people were my high school football coach, Charles Boston; one of my football coaches at Alcorn State, Marino Casem; my roommate at the University of Georgia, Eddie Stone; my boss at Jackson Public Schools, Dr. Robert Fortenberry; and my supervisor of officials in the NFL, Art McNally. Many others, also, helped.

This book is a testament to the goodness of people. It is an opportunity to illustrate and demonstrate what happens when people are allowed to give you help. I never had an idea that I would become an NFL official or president of the state College Board. This book is about capturing those thoughts and putting them into a context to share them with others. The whole goal here is to authenticate that, if you don't give up on a person, the best will come out. This book is not a monument to me; it is a monument to the people who helped me along my journey.

Many of my stories in this book address issues that we are dealing with today. We condemn people without knowing them. We make decisions about people without knowing them. This book shares stories about people who weren't that way. For example, one of those stories is about my University of Georgia roommate, Eddie Stone, who is white. He had never been around black people, but his whole idea about black people's social skills changed because we were able to communicate. As we got to know each other, he learned what I was really like. This book provides me an opportunity to explain this further. I never doubted my ability to cope with the brainwashing and negativity associated with integration or my ability to cope with the turmoil that was prevalent at that time.

I was a student at Alcorn, lying in bed and listening to the radio, as they gave a blow-by-blow about James Meredith getting into Ole Miss. It was a scary time, but, when I got to the University of Georgia, I got a chance to prove that all of those stereotypes were not true. That was when I decided to write this book. It's not something to brag about it. This is about my life. This is about my experiences and how people have molded me along my journey. I hope you enjoy it and can learn from it. I have been extremely blessed by God.

CHAPTER ONE

Family

I was born on November 10, 1941 in Jefferson Davis County. Our family doctor, Dr. Nichols, delivered me at our farm. My brother, the late Dr. Charles Haynes, wrote a book— *Growing Up Colored in Mississippi*—and he did a wonderful job of describing how and where we grew up in rural Jefferson Davis County.

We lived two and a half miles from Carson, out in the hilly countryside, down a gravelly road. Our address was Route 1, Box 238, Carson, Mississippi. Our house was on a graded hill about two hundred feet from the road.

We had a relatively comfortable, seven room farmhouse. It had a large, concrete front porch, the width of the house, that rose about three feet above the ground. There were two front entranceways into the house. Both entranceways had screen doors to keep out the flies and mosquitoes and solid wooden doors to keep out the weather.

The entranceway on the left led first to a guest bedroom, and then to a second bedroom where Mama and Daddy slept. Daddy and Mama's bedroom served as a family room. This was where the black and white television and the fireplace were located. In front of the fireplace was a concrete hearth that jutted out about two feet. On top of the fireplace was a mantelpiece, and on top of the mantelpiece was an old, medium-sized grandfather clock that did not work. It was useless, except as a storage place for a few semi-important papers.

After Daddy and Mama's bedroom, there was a back bedroom where I slept with my two brothers, Charles and Isaac. The other front entranceway led directly to the living room. This living room was more of an ornament than a sitting room because, when we had company, we entertained our guests either in the fireplace room, or, if it was spring or summer, on the front porch.

Off the living room was the dining room where we ate all of our meals. And then there was the kitchen, complete with a large freezer, a butane gas stove, and a refrigerator. Just behind the kitchen was the back porch. Toward the end of my adolescence, half of this back porch was partitioned off to form an indoor toilet. The bathroom contained a sink, a bathtub, and a flushable toilet.

The front of our house faced the east, so the sun's heat washed our front porch nearly every morning. The house was covered from side to side with white asbestos siding, and the roof was green.

The front yard was huge. It sloped gradually downhill to the pebbly road. Off to the right side of the house was a three-acre pasture where we kept our herd of cows at night. Positioned in the middle of this pasture was a fenced-in, wooden lot, and inside this lot was a big barn that was always kept full of hay. The lower portion of the barn contained cribs for storing corn and stables for keeping our horses and mules. We parked our tractor in the barn at night. Chickens and hogs were allowed to roam freely in the lot and out in the holding pasture.

Directly across from the gravelly road—a road that was very dusty when dry and very slippery when wet—that ran in front of our house was our big pasture. During the day, the cows and horses roamed this big pasture and nibbled from the mahalia grass in the hollows. In fact, this pasture was made up of many hills and valleys. In one of the hollows, deeper into the pasture amid a thick cluster of gum and poplar trees, there were several springheads where water bubbled up out of the ground to form a clear water creek where cattle could quench their thirst. The hills and hillsides were wonders to behold. They were cluttered with tall, stately pine trees that Daddy seldom cut. For Daddy, these huge pine trees represented money in the bank and the grand pride of ownership. He let them stand for the world to see, as though the trees were a showcase that said to the world that he was doing all right. Daddy, also, owned a forty-acre plot of timberland over Highway 13 in the western part of the county.

Adjacent to the big pasture to the north was a huge, rolling field that was used on alternate years to plant big crops of cotton and corn. That field was also used to grow smaller crops such as cucumbers, snap beans, watermelons, sweet potatoes, black-eyed peas, and butter beans.

The biggest field of all was located behind the house. Initially, there was only a thirteen-acre field behind the house. This was before Daddy purchased the Ruby place. The Ruby place was previously owned by a white man, Mr. Lewis King.

Back in 1954, when I was thirteen, Mr. King decided to sell his place. Mr. King had placed an advertisement stating that his

forty-five acres of land and farmhouse were for sale for $4,000.
My dad had been looking over the fence at this land for years.
When he heard it was for sale, he approached the owner. There
was a lot of racism back then. Mr. King basically said it was for
sale, but that he wasn't going "to sell it to no nigger". That was
the first approach, but my dad did not give up. He went back
again.

This time, Mr. King said he would sell it to my dad for
$4,500 cash. That was a lot of money back then. Then, suddenly,
he raised the price to $5,000. My dad agonized over it and
wondered why he would sell it for this inflated price. He would
talk about it at the breakfast table. While my dad toyed with the
idea, Mr. King didn't believe my dad could afford to buy the
land, but my dad proved him wrong.

Because my daddy couldn't write out the check, he asked
Mr. King to meet him at the bank. Once at the bank, the banker
wrote the check. The seller, Mr. King, asked the banker if the
check was good, and the banker reassured him, telling him that
it was. (The Bank of Blountville is still standing in Prentiss now,
but it isn't a bank. A photocopy of the check is included in the
photo section of this book).

At this point, Mr. King signed the deed, and everything was
handed over to my dad. My dad was elated that he was able to
buy the land, but he was broke. He didn't have a penny left. He
came to me and told me that we had to make some money. I
believe the Lord was with us because, in two years, we had
earned the money back by farming the extra land. I, now, own
all of the land that my dad owned. I feel a responsibility to keep
it because I understand how important the farm was to him.

*****

My mother and father were the backbones of our education. There were three boys in my family. Isaac, who now lives in Carson, is a tree farmer. He started off as a teacher, but teaching wasn't as profitable as he wanted it to be. He went to Alcorn. Charles went to Alcorn on the same day I did.

My mother's background was in education. She believed in it. She finished high school and college. My dad believed in education, too; however, at times, he would want to keep us out of school to pick cotton or plant corn, but my mother wouldn't let him. Right off the bat, there were differences, but my mother stood firm in her belief in education. Therefore, that was the primary decision for all three of us to attend Alcorn.

My mother had been married before she met my dad. During that marriage, she had a daughter; her name is Ruth Brazand-Baugh. There was a conflict because she was a step-daughter and because she had grown up in a different atmosphere. She had lived with my grandmother in Hattiesburg, Mississippi, so, when she came to the country, it was not a perfect fit. Because of her lifestyle, it created some friction. She was extremely smart like my mom, and an excellent student, but she just never did fit into the farm life. It was routine for us to be up at 5:30, but that wasn't her lifestyle. If you picture a farmer, he doesn't want to see anyone in the bed after 5:30 in the morning. I'm talking about my dad. A natural conflict arose between the two.

When I was young, I didn't understand it, but, as I grew older, I did. She had grown up with my grandmother in a semi-urban environment, close to the airport in Hattiesburg. My mother allowed Ruth to return to my grandmother's to alleviate that situation.

My father was a farmer, and he had grown up on the farm. When it came to school, he had only finished the fifth grade, but he recognized the importance of his kids getting an education. My dad was a man before his time. He was a guy who believed a handshake was a contract. He believed in being on time, and he expected his children to be on time, as well. Once he told us something, that was it; he didn't forget. He was a hard worker.

Like my father, I was acclimated to the farm. I was accustomed to getting up at 5:30 in the morning. In the summertime, we would always look forward to going home and going to the swimming hole with my father. It wasn't very far from the house. While we were all playing around, he would take a nap around noon for five to fifteen minutes. He would take his hat off and be snoring quickly. After the fifteen minute nap, he would grab his hat and say, "Let's get back to the field." He could surely time a nap. He was amazing.

When I was a teacher in Jackson, and he was suffering from emphysema in his late sixties, I would go down to the farm to see him often. I would never disagree with him. If he wanted something trimmed on the fence row, I would do it. Remember, he was a farmer, and farmers can look out over the land and recognize when something needs to be done. It's just an inherent ability that most farmers possess.

So, I would run down to the fence row to complete my assigned task because I didn't have but an hour at the most. I was trying to call baseball games and do all these other activities during this time. He would say, "Joe, you see that limb over there? I want you to cut those limbs hanging over the fence."

I would go and cut them off because I respected my dad so much. I didn't want him to be sitting there, thinking the farm was going to waste. I tried to do everything I could to please him. He'd put his whole life into farming, and he'd done a good job of it. He supplemented his farming income by logging. He was an entrepreneur, even back then.

During lay-by season, he would hire a guy to drive a truck with a long trailer attached to it and would haul things for other people. Lay-by season was a six to eight week period from mid-July to the fall. Before the harvesting started, we would plant the crop in the early spring. Then, we would cultivate the crop and lay it by. After that, we were through until the fall. We would find something else to do, and my dad filled his time by logging.

My dad was not an overly religious person. He would go to church, but he lived his religion. In other words, he always did the right thing; he was fair to everyone. If he owed you, he would pay you back on time. If you owed someone, he would tell you to pay it back on time as well.

For example, when I first started teaching, I made $2,400 a year, more or less. I needed to pay a car note, so my dad signed the note because I didn't have the credit. This was in 1963 or '64. We went to Dumas Milner Chevrolet, located where the post office is now in Jackson, and we bought a car.

Every month, I would run out of money, and I would have to go to my dad and borrow one hundred dollars to pay my car note. And, every month, I would pay him back one hundred dollars. He loaned it to me in the middle of the month, and I paid him back at the end of the month. He did that for a year. The lesson was that you have to be responsible and pay the bills. Even now, if someone wants to upset me, all they have to do is not pay me on time. If they don't pay on time, I have a problem with them. I inherited that from my daddy. He was an honest person.

My dad was, also, extremely frugal. He saved his money, and he didn't believe in handouts. He instilled a superb work ethic in us. He gave us the confidence to believe that we could do anything. I often tell people that I wish every kid could experience life on a farm. Because on the farm, we had to show up every day. We couldn't just say, "I will go out there when I want to." We had to take advantage of what the good Lord had given to us. When the crop came up, we had to fertilize it at the right time. Farming is a lesson in how to be productive and punctual.

Around 1955, my dad and my uncle bought a tractor. I became the operator of the tractor. It was my job to drive it and cultivate the fields. During that time, I learned the value of being punctual and doing the right thing.

One night, there was an end of the year school closing program that I wanted to attend. My dad told me, if I went to that program, I had better be back to work the next day. This was a Friday night, and Saturday was a full workday. I went to the program with my buddy, and on the way home, the fuel pump on his truck went out. As a result, we got home just as the sun was beginning to rise, and I knew there was some important work to be done that day. I had some work to do that required me to use the tractor. Because I hadn't gotten any sleep, I was so tired that I fell asleep on the tractor, ran into a tree, and cracked the radiator. That was when I realized the importance of listening to good common sense. My dad told me not to go to that program, but I went anyway. I learned an important lesson from that experience.

When I was eighteen years old, my dad urged me to register to vote. There were two things he wanted us boys to do—register for the Army and register to vote. When I went to register to vote, I had to interpret certain parts of the U.S. Constitution. I had to write the correct answers in order to be eligible to vote. This was in the late fifties or early sixties.

*****

The education we received at Alcorn was stellar. As I stated earlier, my mother went to school there. Her mother had also attended college, but not at Alcorn. My mother's sister went to Alcorn, and my wife went to Alcorn, as well.

I delivered a speech at Alcorn during graduation the year before President George Bush Sr. was the speaker. I was on the state College Board at the time. My speech was about HBCUs (historically black colleges and universities) and their importance.

When I was on the state College Board, there was an issue about whether we needed Alcorn, Jackson State, and Mississippi Valley State. My speech addressed why we needed these schools. If I had not gone to Alcorn, I wouldn't have finished college. I couldn't go to Southern Miss, Mississippi State, or Ole Miss at that time. At that time, Alcorn—or some other black college—was the only college I could attend.

My wife, Dorothy, played a tremendous role in my success in life. In many situations, whether we agreed or not, she never stopped me from doing what I wanted to do, and she was always extremely supportive of my decisions. I will never forget when I went to Greenville to be the superintendent. Some of her friends couldn't believe she was going to leave her comfortable home in North Jackson and move there, but my wife disagreed with them.

While I was deputy superintendent of Jackson Public Schools, my wife had to take a second seat to a lot of things. My kids grew up in a fish bowl type of environment. Everything they did was scrutinized and held to a higher standard just because of who I was.

Many times, my kids were, also, second. Even during my time in the Southeastern Conference (SEC), my wife was extremely supportive of me. I remember I worked a game between Army and Florida in Gainesville, Florida on a Saturday, and I had a junior varsity game on the following Monday in Nashville. We had a baby then (Kristi), and my wife drove, for the most part, from Gainesville to Nashville. Our baby got sick, and we had to go to the hospital in north Alabama. I was working on my doctorate, and I had preliminary exams that Wednesday, so she drove while I studied. My wife was always there for me. You can't be an official or administrator without family support.

Another example of how my family was involved in my National Football League (NFL) officiating career was when I officiated a game between the 49ers and the New York Jets at Candlestick Park in San Francisco. My wife and the kids went with me on this trip. I was deputy superintendent of JPS, and I had to be back at work on Monday. My wife and kids had not had the opportunity to get out and see the sights, so they left the game at halftime in order to enjoy San Francisco some before we had to leave.

FAMILY MEMBERS

DOROTHY KENNEDY HAYNES
We have been married for more than forty-nine years. She and I met during the spring of my senior year in college and were married a year later. We both taught school in Pinola, Mississippi during the early years of our educational career. Dorothy worked as a business education teacher, and I worked as a football coach and teacher. Additionally, she was employed at Jackson State University, Madison County School District, and Callaway High School for a total of fifteen years. During this time, she became certified as a computer programming instructor with certification in business and computer technology. In addition, she holds a Bachelor's of Science Degree, Master's of Science Degree, and an educational specialist's degree.

As both our educational careers flourished, I was selected to be a superintendent in Greenville. After the second year of being superintendent, our district was selected to participate in a pilot project known as the Technology Preparation Program. The program needed guidance and structure. Because of my wife's vast knowledge base when it came to computers, she was asked to serve as the technology consultant. While working among teachers and administrative personnel, training in technology was given to other school employees, as well as other school districts in the Mississippi Delta. The Greenville community gives her credit for the outstanding implementation of the Technology Preparation Program and for her unending dedication to seeing it get done.

Many of her students excelled in the field of technology and, today, are employed by leading corporations in America in areas such as computer engineering, computer science, and programming, as well as opening their own computer-related businesses.

Currently, she is happy being a grandmother, holding church membership, and participating in various civic and social organizations—one of which celebrated its centennial in Washington, D.C. in July 2013. She especially enjoys visiting with family and childhood friends who live throughout the United States.

Dorothy and I are the proud parents of two children, Joe Christopher and Kristi Lanet'. Christopher presently works in state education, and Kristi is a registered nurse. She has two wonderful daughters, Erriona and Kristion, both of whom excel academically. Erriona is sixteen, and Kristion is six. I find them to be a lot of fun, and they are always very anxious to keep me up-to-date on the latest gadgets, music hits, and musical idols.

ISAAC HAYNES

He is the baby in the family, the youngest of the three boys. He graduated from Carver High School and played football there. Isaac graduated from Alcorn State and became a teacher. However, due to the low salary, he decided to go into business for himself as a tree surgeon, and he has been involved in timber management for many years.

DR. CHARLES HAYNES

He is the middle child in our family. He graduated from Carver High School and Alcorn State. He taught in Alaska after graduating from Alcorn and decided to continue his education. He received his master's and doctorate degrees in psychology from the University of Arizona. He also taught at the University of Florida and University of Wisconsin and is the author of three books.

ISAAC HAYNES SR.

This is my father's brother, and their favorite pastime was talking about how favorable the crops looked during the lay-by time during the summer. Just like my parents, my uncle believed in education. His wife was a teacher. They have three daughters — two graduated from Alcorn State, and the other one from Tougaloo College in Jackson.

FLORA HAYNES-BOOTH

My mother taught school for thirty-eight years in Jefferson Davis County. Education was her life. She volunteered to teach reading after she retired. She was a music teacher at several churches over the years in our community. However, her greatest contribution to our family was her persistence that all of her children get an education.

ALLEN HAYNES

My father was a farmer that believed in working twelve hour days. He expected his sons to do the same. He was ahead of his time because of his entrepreneurial talents. It was very important to him for people to pay on time and to be honest. That trait was filtered down to his children.

RUTH BRAZAND-BAUGH
My sister, Ruth, grew up in Hattiesburg, Mississippi where she lived with my grandmother.

CHAPTER TWO

Faith

When I was a child, I was a junior deacon at my church. I had various responsibilities at Hollis Creek Baptist Church in Carson, Mississippi in Jefferson Davis County. It taught me to walk right and that a lot was expected of me. If I didn't go to Sunday school, I felt guilty, and, when I worked on Sundays, I felt guilty. Going to church kept me in line, and it brought me back to reality.

As I ventured out into the world, I seemed to be at the right place at the right time, and I got along with everybody. Because of what I learned in Sunday School and, later, in church, when they were looking for the right guys to join the Mississippi High School Activities Association officials and leave the Magnolia Association, I was chosen, and I felt it was necessary to step up. As one of the first black officials in the SEC and the first black football official in the Mississippi Junior College Association, it was very important not to let my emotions get out of control. There were the social issues and the success, and I had to get along with everybody. My faith played a big part in that. It also played a big part when I got a chance to get a job with a major company when I was nineteen years old.

I was given a chance with the Brown-Miller Pickle Company. Earl Holloway gave me an opportunity that I will never forget and have never been able to repay him for. This was the 1960s, and I was given a leadership role over some white guys, and they accepted me. Even then, I was recognized for my ability and not the color of my skin.

Because I was an NFL official, I was gone a lot of Sundays, but I didn't want to lose contact with the Farish Street Baptist Church, which I joined in 1968. On Sundays, when I was home, it was a blessing to be able to go to church at Farish Street Baptist. It gave me a peaceful feeling. I enjoyed the questions about being a referee from others in the congregation. They followed me when I was refereeing.

HOME FOLKS IN GEORGIA

When I was going to graduate school at the University of Georgia, I wanted to get a feeling of home, so I decided to go to church there. It was the appeal of my upbringing, and I missed the people in my home church. The people I encountered in Georgia were religious and faith-based, just like those back home. They were friendly, too. I was a long way from home, and I was looking for people with similar thoughts and values. It was a connector for me.

MY FAITH IN THE NFL

At one of our NFL officials' pre-game conferences, Bob Wagner would have a devotional and give his testimony. Sometimes, one of the other referees would give theirs. The devotional meant a lot to all of us. It made us ready for the game. Before the game, we would have some dead time. Fred, our referee, would do funny things to try and keep everyone loose. I would sneak away and pray in the restroom. I was so thankful. Only God could take a man from the cotton rows of Carson, Mississippi, and put him on the field at an NFL game with 50,000 or more people watching. The Good Lord put me there, and praying was a way of saying thank you.

I knew that I had to trust my faith while I was working a game, and the NFL had to trust me and believe that I would do a good job. When I prayed, it was like a weight was taken off my shoulders. God took the pressure off of me and put it on Himself. During a game between the Eagles and Giants, I got on my knees at Franklin Field before kickoff and asked God to protect me and help me do my job to the best of my ability. The Good Lord was always there with me.

*****

"Joe and I first met when I was working in the Big Eight Conference. Joe and I officiated a Kentucky and Oklahoma game together," Bob Wagner said. "Joe was on my crew for four years in the NFL, and he is a fine gentleman. As a crew, we would get together and have devotionals on Sunday mornings. We felt it was important to seek a greater power and draw together as men of faith. God is much greater than our stripes or our position as referees, and we needed to recognize that fact with our worship of Him.

"Our devotionals took a lot of the pressure off of us and put the direction of pressure toward a Higher Power. It was comforting to defuse that pressure. We would pray that men would rally around the right things and perform better and respect coaches, players, and officials. We hoped they would respond in a kind way and not in anger. It is so important, during the heat of the battle, that coaches, players, and officials be careful with the use of their tongue and keep their composure. I could always tell what men were Christians by the way they acted and would rally around the right things. Joe is definitely a strong Christian and a powerful man of faith. There were all kinds of challenges on and off the field for us as officials, and our devotionals and prayer time helped unlock that tension and helped us deal with all of it."

*****

A FOCUSED DEACON

Our pastor had faith in us young deacons and said our faith had to grow. I was thirty years old when I became a deacon. I knew older people might criticize me, but I had to live above the fray. Having now been a deacon for thirty plus years, I've realized a few things. If you are not careful, you can collect some baggage. If you are not careful, it will throw you. If you don't stay focused, it will derail you.

We had a split in our church, and there was a lady in the church that wouldn't speak to me. I didn't know what I did. She had always been cheerful, but, all of a sudden, she went into a shell, all because I disagreed with her. My wife and I decided that our faith had to be stronger than our church building, and we resolved our issues. Our pastor had started when he was twenty-nine years old and has been there for forty plus years.

REVEREND HICKMAN JOHNSON: "JOE TAKES HIS FAITH SERIOUSLY"

"Joe is a natural leader. He has served as chairman of our deacons and on the board of trustees. He is able to encourage others to follow," said Rev. Hickman Johnson, who has served as pastor for more than forty plus years at the Farish Street Baptist Church in Jackson. "My wife was a librarian at Jackson State University and used to work at Siwell Junior High School when Joe was principal there. I have followed his career in and outside of education. Our members seek advice from Joe and look up to him. I feel Joe has earned the respect of his fellow church members. I am extremely pleased at Joe's growth in his faith and how he has matured from a young man to become one of the leaders of our church. He is able to lead our worship and shares the role of a spiritual leader. Our deacons alternate in leading worship, prayer, and scripture reading. He doesn't mind sharing his testimony. When he wasn't appointed as superintendent of Jackson Public Schools, he handled it well and bounced back. Joe continued to give to the community. He worked his way up to that logical step. He may have been quick tempered in his early life, but he has matured and learned how to walk away. He has modified his own temper, and he has matured in his faith. Joe is a go-getter. He's just not concerned about his career and money. Joe has something to offer and is always looking for ways to contribute. Joe grew up in modest circumstances, and he has an obligation to give back and pass it forward. He takes his faith seriously. I have taught a sermon series on 'The Sermon on the Mount,' and I talk about how we need to learn how to live. Joe knows how. That's what I see in Joe Haynes."

PART II

EDUCATIONAL PURSUITS

CHAPTER THREE

Jackson Public Schools

Dr. Robert Fortenberry was the superintendent of Jackson Public Schools for seventeen years, from 1973-1990, and helped the largest school system in Mississippi deal with the difficult years of desegregation. He is well-known across the country and knows a great educator when he sees one. I am honored that he saw immediately me as one. Dr. Fortenberry came to Jackson in 1973 when I was an assistant principal at Provine.

*****

"Joe is one of the most remarkable people that I have gotten to know in my life and one of the people who has had a significant influence on what I've done and what I've been able to accomplish," Dr. Fortenberry said. "He has had a tremendous influence on my life. We are not going to make progress in this nation until we recognize the deep and continuing curse of racism in the country. Joe has helped a number of people understand the impact of racism without being an individual who is bitter and critical. He has been able to help all of us come to grips with the fact of who we are because he has been able to distinguish between those who continue to be racist and those who are not. There are many African-Americans who maintain their own position, but Joe has never done that because he understands why we must move beyond that point. He has done many significant things in his continuing career in education, in his SEC and NFL football officiating years, and as president of the College Board in Mississippi. He has a lot of firsts, but those are not his most significant contributions. Joe's most significant contributions are his honesty, his integrity, and his ability to help all of us understand why we must work together in honesty. He has been able to facilitate that, not only with whites, but also with a lot of blacks.

"I recognized two things when I first became superintendent in Jackson. First of all, I recognized that there was a good group of older people, who came out of the old system, who were never allowed to make decisions. Some, because of race; some, because of other things, and I had to identify a group of younger people, those who were emerging, those who had immediately come through the process of desegregation as a primary force to help me improve that school system. And Joe was one of the educators that I identified early on.

"We built Siwell Road Junior High School, which, at that time, was 65-70 percent white when it opened. I asked Joe if he would take that job as the first principal of that school. And he said, 'Well, I don't know whether I should or not. Will they give me a chance there?' I said, 'I think so. I think we can help that happen.' Joe said, 'I can make it if they give me a chance.' And he did. He didn't stay there long."

*****

I felt that I was doing a good job as the principal at Siwell, but I had a few problems confronting me. One of the most important advantages of being the first principal at Siwell was that I had the pick of all the high school and junior high school teachers in Jackson. I had an expert in everything. I had a good student council director. I had a good social studies department chair and good math teachers. In other words, all I had to do was be a good leader.

We had had a successful school year at Siwell when we ended that May. At the beginning of June, I received a call out of the clear blue. It was Dr. Fortenberry.

"Hey, Joe," he said. "Come to my office."

When you get a call from your boss to come to his office, it causes concern, especially at the end of the school year. After I arrived at his office, he told me that he wanted me to take over the transportation department for Jackson Public Schools. During the school year, we'd had some trouble in the transportation area. We had just gone from kids walking to school to picking them up a mile from home. We had 325 busses that ran every day. Dr. Fortenberry wanted me to be transportation director. I was the principal of this new school with state of the art facilities. It was the best school in Jackson at that time. I immediately said no without thinking. He said okay. That was the end of the conversation. I left and was happy that I didn't take the job. He didn't speak to me for a week about that subject.

The next week, Dr. Fortenberry called a meeting of all the junior high and high school principals at his office. He went around the room and asked everyone in the room, "If you were transportation director, what would you do?"

When it was my turn, he skipped me. He was really playing a game with me then. He told me after the meeting that I didn't have any answers. Well, that kind of concerned me since it was coming from my boss.

*****

Dr. Fortenberry said, "There was a bus driver's strike in Jackson. Well, it wasn't really a strike; they just said they were going to stay home. I looked around the school district to see who was here with knowledge and integrity to do this job, and I identified Joe. I called all the principals together and went around the room and asked them what I should do. I called on Joe last. Then, I asked him if he would take the job, and he told me no, because he had a good job. It was true, he had a good job, and he was doing an awesome job there."

*****

One Sunday morning, I was getting ready to go to church. I picked up the newspaper and noticed a story about JPS considering hiring a new transportation director. I immediately picked up the phone and called Dr. Fortenberry because I felt the need to be a team player. I said to him, "Dr. Fortenberry, we can talk Monday, but I'll take the job." I hung up the phone. I arrived at his office Monday; we talked about the job, and he put me in charge of transportation.

Said Dr. Fortenberry, "Joe immediately saw the situation. He was very insightful. He got all the administrators a bus driving certificate, so they could drive the busses, and that sent a significant message. That proved his knowledge and his worth."

We needed support from the principals to help the drivers with some of their issues in running their bus routes. The principals realized that they could do more to help the drivers do their job after they recognized they were going to have to go to training themselves.

Dr. Fortenberry added me to the administrative cabinet, where a lot of the important decisions were made for the district for board approval. Some of the administrators questioned his decision to put a new person, who also had voting power, at the cabinet level. Since I was just a novice, I could understand their concern. I received an $11,000 raise. Dr. Fortenberry gave me so much encouragement, and, from then on, my whole career centered on his involvement with me. He used to give me some very difficult assignments. There were some days I went away thinking, Why would he want to do this to me?

I had worked with transportation successfully. I was a young administrator at the time. I was able to eliminate the negative talk about transportation. "Squeal on Wheels" was a slogan on the back of all the busses, which had a number that could be called if a bus driver was driving poorly. I pulled all of those slogans off the busses. That was one of the first things I did. That improved moral because the bus drivers didn't like the fact that someone could call and make a complaint about their driving. I called the bus drivers in and told them I was taking the slogan off, "but, in return, *you've* got to do the right thing." And guess what? They did do the right thing, and all the negative stuff went away. People couldn't believe it. All it took was developing a good relationship with the drivers.

Dr. Fortenberry also gave me the responsibility of being in charge of the finance office. I was not an accountant; however, I could balance my own checkbook. We were getting ready to go from a manual system to an automated system. We had people in the finance office who were qualified to do the financial planning, but it was my job to manage these people. To the average person, questions arose about my ability to do this job. There were television reporters, radio personalities, and investigative reporters who put the camera right on me and asked me what I knew about finance.

While Wydette Hawkins of Channel 12 was interviewing me and the camera was rolling, I asked him to please turn off the camera. I wanted to talk about it off camera first. I explained to him that I didn't think I was appointed to the finance office to balance the budget or do the accounting. I was there to deal with the personalities that we had in the finance office. I told Mr. Hawkins, before he broadcasted the information, that I wanted him to do some background work. I wanted him to go to Provine, Hardy, Siwell, or to a student or teacher who knew how I had dealt with people and, then, we would talk on camera. He did that and did a good job with the report. He's my friend to this day. Not only did he find out I could work with these people and get them to do the job, he also found out that I could get it done with their support. What I did was recognize human beings. I helped people in that office come together. We had programmers and accountants. I didn't know anything about that, but I knew about human nature. I guarantee you.

We got it done. What I was able to do was take everybody's talents and use them without them blowing up and being too progressive.

*****

"I was director of public affairs at Channel 12 and also worked in the news department. I kept folks informed," Wydette Hawkins said. "I didn't duck or dodge any subject. We took on hot issues—race, education, you name it. Dr. Haynes was appointed to head up several departments, and my position was that he was in charge of big budgets, but he didn't have an accounting or finance background. Most of the time, someone who is in charge of a department like that would have an accounting or finance background. He was dealing with public money. It would have an impact on children's welfare. I questioned his position and his ability to perform the job. Dr. Haynes wasn't happy with me. 'You don't think I can handle it?' he asked. You need to have the best to do this job. I did some background and checked on him. Dr. Haynes stood up for what he believed in. He is serious minded. Dr. Haynes is an icon. He drove me to respect him more. Dr. Haynes has always been effective. He wore his hat backwards. In other words, Dr. Haynes could see what was going on from any direction. He is a giant in our community."

*****

Dr. Fortenberry reorganized his central office. He wanted to put an integrated team together to head up the district.

"I talked to Joe and Dan Merritt about taking those jobs," Dr. Fortenberry said. "It took a while. I had to let some other people retire or encourage them to retire to put together a team of black and white people. Joe took over the operations side, and Dan Merritt took over the instructional side. We had some very interesting reactions. The individual who was in charge of finance wore a cap over his eyes and certainly did not want to go to the use of technology because he had all the figures in his head and on the books. He also told me he would never work for a black person, but he didn't use the word 'black'. I talked to him, and I talked to Joe. I was honest about it. Joe said, 'We will work with that.' He took on that challenge, and it was an extremely important one because, for the first time, the knowledge of finances became generally known by a top level administrator. Prior to that time, I didn't know what the investments were, didn't know what the salaries of people were, all of those kind of things. Joe was the first to help me get those issues straightened out.

"We made the decision—we were one of the first in America—to ask the court to take us from out of the desegregation order. We needed to send the message that, no, that's not the reasons we were doing things in Jackson Public Schools. We were doing it because it was the right thing to do. Most of the black leadership in Jackson was opposed to us getting out from under the court order because they didn't have enough faith in us to do what was right. And justifiably so, because that was not the history. We made the decision, and the board approved it, I believe it was a four to one vote, to seek getting out from under the court order. And that was a very challenging step for the

African-American leadership in the school system because they had to take on the black leadership in the school district.

"I remember there was a gathering of the black leadership that came to see us and met with Joe and me. And we made several steps along the way to get to fairness in the school district, including a commitment to have fifty percent white and fifty percent black employment in the school system. There were several individuals from Jackson State who gave us a hard time in the meeting. About halfway through the meeting, Dr. Haynes asked me to step outside for a minute. In a few minutes, he came and got me, and the people were leaving. I said, 'Joe, what did you tell them?' He said, 'You want to know?' I said, 'Yes, I really want to know.' He said, 'I told them that my you-know-what is just as black as yours, and we are going to do what's right in this school system, and you might as well make up your mind that we are going to do what's right. Whenever y'all get to the position where we are, come back to see us, but, until then, take your politics somewhere else.' That was a very brave thing for Joe to do because he took on the education and community leadership that had every reason to be suspicious of us, but Joe and I knew, at that time, that we were going to make decisions based on what we thought was right for children, regardless of race. I think that was a turning point in what we did.

"Another significant thing we did, in which Joe was very involved, was to have schools in Jackson not identified along racial lines based on who the principal was. If the school was formerly a white school, it would have a white administrative staff, and if it was a formerly black school, it would have a black administrative team there. Also, there was a lot of structural nepotism. There were a whole lot of people in the school who were related to the principal. We decided that, in order to send an appropriate message to the community and the staff, we were going to do whatever it took to focus on the education of children, rather than that of the individual who ran the school according to race. We went up for a retreat to Lake Tiak-O'Khata with a small group of central administrators less than a month before school opened.

"We transferred about ninety percent of the principals. We sent a lot of African-Americans to the suburbs and a lot of whites to the inner city. As you might imagine, there was a lot of discussion in the community. One principal was eventually fired over that because he told us he was not going. Once again, Joe Haynes stood up to the community and school district and said this was an important step to the school district and something we must do.

"Forest Hill became a part of the school district when it was incorporated into the city. Their theme song was 'Dixie' and their flag was the rebel flag. We put together a shared committee to address that issue. Joe was extremely instrumental in getting that accepted. I could recount where Joe had to make decisions on issues in the school district and the message we were trying to send. Now, these were things that were directly related to the way children were perceived and treated. If you set high expectations for kids and help them attain those expectations, they will generally achieve it. We had to present examples of what it took to get to that point. Joe was there, along with several other African-Americans and other whites, to get it done.

"We had a wildcat teacher strike in Jackson. In the early 1980s, many of the administrators outside of the Jackson area supported the teachers in the teachers' strike. Joe, Dan Meritt, and I got together and had a long discussion, and we decided it was primarily our job to keep the schools open, and it was a joint decision. We decided, with legal help, to ask the state board to file an injunction, but they wouldn't do it. It was the decision of the state board and state superintendent that it was a local issue and not a state issue. So, we filed the injunction, with strong support from the Board of Education. Joe and Dan organized the group, and we met at the central office on a Saturday, and the subpoenas were issued to the leadership of both groups out in the state and some in Jackson, and those were delivered that day. We could not have those things if we had been divided racially. Then, we began to really concentrate on what it took to help the students of the Jackson Public Schools. That's the real story of who Joe Haynes is. It's, also, the story of the trust we had. It is a story of his integrity. He is well-known across the country."

CHAPTER FOUR

Provine High School Days

I came to Provine High in the fall of 1971 from Brinkley High, where I had been a teacher and became an assistant principal. Although my role at Provine was assistant principal, I was more of a disciplinarian for Principal Louie Odom. I was an assistant principal at Provine from 1971-1976 and learned from two completely different styles in Principals Louie Odom and Paul McArdle.

Jackson Public Schools were still in the growing pains of integration, and Provine was right in the middle of it. In fact, Provine might have been the most difficult situation because the school was basically half-white and half-black, an almost perfect mix for racial tension. There were students who were bussed from Presidential Hills and Georgetown, both black neighbor-hoods, and there were many who didn't like each other. And then, when the white kids were mixed in, that caused plenty of problems. But I was able to control the situation at Provine, and I influenced hundreds of students during my tenure. Following are some of the students I influenced.

LARRY LOVE: "JOE LET ME TELL MY SIDE OF THE STORY"

When I was an assistant principal at Provine High School, Larry Love was one of the biggest troublemakers in the school. He didn't like anybody. I used to call him into my office often and talk to him for, at least, ten minutes. I used to walk around with his schedule in my pocket because I knew, if there was a fight going on, Larry was going to be involved in it. If someone yelled "Fight! Fight!", most of the time, Larry was fighting with someone. Larry didn't trust anybody, especially me. He thought I was the administration and that I didn't care about him. This was during his junior year. The average person would have given up on this young man, but I didn't.

"Joe truly cared about the students at Provine. He handled things differently," Larry said. "Joe called me to his office one day and said, 'Larry, you've got to find a different way to do things.' I looked at Joe and said, 'I don't trust you.' Then, I got up and left. From our perspective, Joe was an Uncle Tom. That was a very limited perspective because Joe had a genuine concern for our well-being. That attitude was not shared by some of the teachers. One of the teachers and I had a confronta-tion. Joe not only chastised me, but he also chastised the teacher. Joe let me tell my side of the story.

"Joe said recently that I had an impact on his life. That brought tears to my eyes. Being a sixteen or seventeen-year-old kid, you have no sense of that because you are caught up in your own thing. I was, to put it mildly, militant. That's how I was perceived. I was an angry person. The year before Joe came to Provine, we had had a school-wide, racially motivated fight. I was handcuffed and arrested. People thought I had started it.

The next year, Joe showed up. It was as much symbolic as it was an effort to keep a lid on things. His imposing presence and his experience in coaching helped to alleviate the situation. Even though the environment was often as violent and charged as the times were, we were still kids. We had no idea what it must have been like to be Joe Haynes. He was thrown into that situation as much as we were. No one was prepared for all of that."

Larry started coming around in his senior year. In fact, I bought his cap and gown for him. It was eighteen dollars. One of my proudest days was watching him graduate at the Mississippi Coliseum in 1974.

The FBI came to the school to investigate his background. He had applied for the Navy and wanted to be on a submarine. That was top secret stuff, and they wanted to know all about him. The principal sent the FBI to me, and they wanted to know about him. I wasn't going to hide anything.

I said, "He's a smart kid, but he's volatile. I gained his confidence, and I trust him. I think he'll do a good job."

Every time he comes to Jackson, he looks me up.

GREG TREVILLION: "DR. HAYNES HAD THE PULSE OF THE KIDS"

Greg Trevillion was one of the best athletes at Provine when he was there. He admired me and wanted to grow up to be like me. He is now an assistant principal at Madison Middle School in Madison Parish in Tallulah, Louisiana. Greg's father, Dr. Joseph Trevillion, was an assistant superintendent when I was a deputy superintendent in Jackson Public Schools. Greg was an assistant principal and principal in Texas for twenty-three years before moving to Louisiana. He believes I shaped his life while he was a student at Provine from 1974-1977.

"It was a tumultuous time at Provine. There were changing neighborhoods, changing teachers, and changing schools, but Dr. Haynes led us through all of the changes with tremendous leadership," Greg said. "He had the pulse of the kids. Dr. Haynes was right there with us. He was always offering support and encouragement. It was the first time in my life — and, also, in many of the students' lives at Provine — that an administrator had taken the time to listen to us. He also had a heart for the tougher guys, the ones who tried to bully everyone. Dr. Haynes would take the time to talk to them and get them to understand that that wasn't the thing to do and that they needed to respect everyone. He encouraged many kids to go to college. You didn't want to disappoint Dr. Haynes. He kept us together. You could go to sleep and rest assured that Dr. Haynes would take care of the situation. When he said he was going to do something, he did it."

Greg remembered that, when he was in the eleventh grade and was involved in a race fight, I took charge.

"There was a white guy who weighed about 240 pounds. Dr. Haynes told me to get back, but the white guy continued to fight. Dr. Haynes lifted him off the ground. He didn't throw him down or against the wall or anything like that; he just lifted him up and told him to stop fighting," Greg said. "Dr. Haynes had a way of getting your attention without hollering or yelling or using violence. He didn't raise his voice. When he told you to do something, you'd better do it. Dr. Haynes was the type who was always around. He didn't just stay behind a desk or in his office. Dr. Haynes was out in the halls, in the cafeteria, in the gym, in the classroom. He made sure we were acting right and not getting into trouble. Dr. Haynes had a pair of binoculars. Westland Plaza was a shopping center across the street from Provine, and there were students who skipped class and went to Kentucky Fried Chicken over there. He would use those binoculars to find out who was skipping. You didn't get away with much with Dr. Haynes."

Greg was 6'4", 120 pounds as a sophomore basketball player at Provine, but was developed by Coach Harrison Hal into an all-star and averaged almost eighteen points per game as a senior. Greg was so good that Grambling State University in Louisiana signed him to a basketball scholarship. After two seasons, Greg transferred to Tougaloo College in Jackson and finished with honors in elementary education. He graduated from the University of Southern Mississippi with a master's degree in 1984.

"I wanted to be like Dr. Haynes," Greg said.

And he was on his way. Greg was in JPS for five years, coaching for three at Lanier, before leaving for Texas in 1986. Greg's mother, Audrey, worked with my wife, Dorothy, at Callaway High in Jackson for many years. Greg's success makes me feel extremely proud.

DONNIE RHYMES: "JOE HAYNES WAS LIKE CREAM IN A COOKIE"

Donnie Rhymes was a self-proclaimed activist, who was always stirring up trouble at Provine during the early 1970s. Although Donnie didn't finish his senior year at Provine because he was kicked out of school, he received his GED, went to college in California, and earned his master's degree. He joined the Army in 1973 and retired in 1995. Donnie now teaches elementary school in a low income area in Dallas. He has been married for thirty-two years, and he and his wife's only child is a police officer in Dallas. Donnie is another student that I turned around. In fact, Donnie says that I saved his life. Let Donnie tell you how.

"If it hadn't been for Joe Haynes, I would have been gone a long time ago," Donnie said. "He is a good guy and very well-respected. Joe Haynes is an icon. My parents and I look up to him. He is a hardworking man, and he had a tough, tough job at Provine. It was a difficult time back then. There was a lot of racial tension going on and riots like at Penn State and Kent State.

"I was somewhat of an activist. I was very vocal. Someone had to speak up, and that was me. I couldn't understand why all of this conflict was going on. My dad was in the military, and I grew up in a very diverse environment. I had a lot of white friends. I didn't see the color thing at all; I wasn't there. It was a terrible situation. I wasn't going to take verbal abuse from anyone—students or teachers. My parents were conservative, and they even realized something had to be done. I don't regret what I did. I remember Gloria, whose brother was murdered at Jackson State, sitting in art class and crying every day.

"Joe Haynes was a calming force in all of the tension. He is like the cream in a cookie. He always made things right. He always gave me the right advice. He never gave up on me. He never turned his back on me, and I say that from the bottom of my heart. Joe Haynes was always there to stand up for us.

"When I was in the military, we would watch NFL games on TV, and I would see Joe Haynes refereeing, and I would tell everyone that he was a great man and was my assistant principal at Provine. I would always brag about him."

BUTCH TOWNSEND: "I WANTED A RING LIKE JOE HAYNES HAD"

Butch Townsend was one of the white guys who played football at Provine. In the spring of 1972, I was helping coach football, and Butch was going through spring practice. Butch respected me and listened intently to my instructions about football and how to play the game. One day, Butch noticed something different about me. Specifically, my right hand.

"I saw a gigantic class ring on his finger. It was from the University of Georgia (where Dr. Haynes received his master's degree)," Butch said. "It was a beautiful ring. He took it off, and I put it on my finger. I told Dr. Haynes, 'I sure would like to have a ring like that one day.' He told me to 'buckle down and apply myself, and I could get one.' I went home and told my dad about it and how he wouldn't believe how big it was. We weren't poor, but we weren't rich, and my dad told me we had never had anyone in our family to go to college, much less graduate. My dad said, if I finished college, that he would buy me one of those rings. I went to the bookstore a few weeks before I graduated (from the University of Southern Mississippi) to look for the ring I wanted. I really liked one called 'the heritage ring', but it had a small diamond in it, and it was really expensive. They said they could replace it with cubic zirconia, and it would cheaper, so I thought my dad might go for that. I told him about it, and he said he didn't want me to have a fake diamond. He wanted me to have the real thing. It was a few hundred dollars more, and that was a lot back then. I still wear it to this day."

Butch, who is now the public relations director of the City of Pearl police department, remembers me as a well-dressed man with traits of honesty and fairness.

"Dr. Haynes didn't single out students," Butch said. "We weren't too far removed from desegregation, and tensions were still somewhat high. Dr. Haynes was fair, regardless of race."

Butch was one of those guys who I caught making a poor decision.

"We had a physical education class in sixth period, and some of us would slip away from school after that and go off campus to the Totesum convenience store down the road," Butch said. "One day, we were standing in line to check out, and I felt a big presence behind me. It was Dr. Haynes. He said, 'Townsend, see me when you get back to campus.' Dr. Haynes was stern, but fair — a great role model. I also told my friends about Dr. Haynes when I would see him on TV refereeing in the NFL. I told them to watch for No. 112. That was Dr. Haynes."

DEBRA STRINGFELLOW: "MR. HAYNES WAS TOUGH, BUT FAIR."

Debra Stringfellow's family, which included five kids, loved me. I lived in the Stringfellow's neighborhood and would give their children rides to school. Debra graduated from Provine in 1974. Clintorice, graduated from Provine in 1973, and Eric graduated from Provine in 1978.

"Mr. Haynes was a great person. Now, he was tough, but he was fair," Debra said. "He stood up for the kids. When someone would do something wrong, he would take care of them, he listened to them, too. We had a lot of respect for him.

"One of the times when I saw Mr. Haynes get really angry was when someone popped firecrackers on the school bus on our way home. The bus driver called Mr. Haynes, and he parked the bus until Mr. Haynes got there. Mr. Haynes got on the bus and was really angry. He gave us a nice lecture, like he was a preacher. But we deserved it. It didn't happen again."

CARLA NICKS: "YOU NEVER CROSSED DR. HAYNES"

Carla Nicks was involved when she attended Provine and graduated early in 1979. She was named Most Beautiful. She was a drum major, a beauty, a Hall of Famer, a Class Capers designer, on the yearbook staff, and on the homecoming court.

She went on to be a Hinds Community College Hi-Stepper and was the first black Miss Hinds in 1980. Seven years later, she was named the first black Mrs. Mississippi. She has been with UPS for twenty-six years and is the human resource specialist.

"Dr. Haynes was very stern and strict. He was a disciplinarian," Carla said. "He worked the halls. Dr. Haynes had a reputation of good fear. He kept order. He was truly fair. He earned respect. You didn't cross the line, and you never crossed him. He had the respect of the faculty. He had the assurance of the administration and the community. He would bring in mentors and speakers and had amazing connections with the community. One of those mentors he brought in was Mrs. Alon Bee, the head of the Hinds Community College Hi-Steppers. She was my mentor in the fashion club and was a celebrity to me because I used to watch her on TV. Dr. Haynes instilled in us the importance of staying out of trouble. He had a personal interest in each of us and knew the value of knowing every student. He wanted to save us from our mistakes, but, if we made mistakes, he would listen to us. He was known as 'Joe Blow' around school because his blow with the paddle would singe. You heard the bang through the school."

ELLEN AREGOOD: "MR. HAYNES WAS BIGGER THAN LIFE"

Ellen Aregood was Miss Provine and vice-president of the student body. She graduated from Provine in 1973 and admits she was a Miss Goody Two-Shoes.

"Mr. Haynes was bigger than life. He was firm, but he was fun," Ellen said. "Some people called him 'Smokin' Joe'. You didn't mess with him. He always had a big smile on his face. He and Mr. Odom ran a tight ship. It was hard when we first went into Provine, the year after desegregation. We forced good friendships and have good memories from those days. I still have friends from Provine thirty years later. Certainly, there was tension, but I was never frightened. It was hard trying to get to know people who were different from me and who came from different neighborhoods and backgrounds, but it was a good experience. I know, in Class Capers, we had a good time and color didn't matter. I remember my high school days as a fun time in my life, and Dr. Haynes was a big part of why it was fun."

CHAPTER FIVE

Hardy Junior High and Siwell Junior High

(Kids at Hardy Skipping)

While I was principal at Hardy Middle School, we had kids riding the bus who would get off in the morning and run straight through Hughes Field (Jackson Public School's football field, which was on Hardy's campus) to Westland Plaza Shopping Center (a few hundred yards from the school). There was a McRae's, Super D, Jitney Jungle and other stores. The managers of those stores were giving me a very hard time about these students coming into their stores. I called a faculty meeting and said, "Look, we've got to stop this."

I assigned teachers to different posts around the school each morning. I gained a few enemies because some of the teachers just wanted to sit in the lounge, and they didn't want to do what I assigned them to do.

I called in my classes and had a talk. We had had about six weeks of school so far, and we had about twenty violators. But that talk didn't help them. I brought in a few of the leaders who were causing trouble. They were tough guys. I brought them into my office and told them to get some candy. I asked them,

"What do I need to do to stop you guys from skipping school? You guys are making my reputation bad."

They stopped doing it. They would help me to keep other people from running to Westland Plaza. Jason was a student who was bad news. One of the teachers came up to me and asked what was I doing to him. I said, "What?"

She said he was coming to class on time. If I saw this student in the hallway doing something good, I would praise him, and his whole attitude changed. The fact that I gave him credit for doing something good gave him confidence and made him feel better about himself.

I was often surprised by what a difference it made when my students received praise for doing things the right way. It motivated them and gave them the energy and ability to go forward, but they needed us to praise them and encourage them.

THE MOVE FROM HARDY TO SIWELL

I thought I was doing a good job as the principal at Hardy Junior High, but Dr. Tom Taylor, the assistant superintendent of JPS, showed up at school one day in early February. I hadn't seen him all day. He walked down the hall and looked around. I didn't really know what was going on, but I found out when Dr. Fortenberry called me into his office downtown. Dr. Fortenberry wanted me to be the first principal at Siwell Road Junior High School, a new school on Highway 18 in South Jackson. Dr. Fortenberry had sent his advance team, which included Dr. Tom Taylor, to check me and Hardy out, to see what kind of job I was doing.

I went down to Siwell to get all the details. The good thing about the new school was that it had wall-to-wall carpet and very few windows. It was really nice. The bad part was that I had to start over with teachers, but the good part was that I got to choose my teachers. I was going to have the pick of the district. We had more than 2,000 teachers, and I could pick anyone I wanted. All they had to do was apply. Then, I would interview them and make my selection. It was kind of like picking a football team, and I knew who the stars were.

One of the stars I picked was Jane Bryan. Mrs. Bryan had worked with me at Hardy. She was an exceptional reading teacher. When I got to Hardy, I had to clean that place up, and Mrs. Bryan was extremely supportive of how I did that. She was always on her job, doing her job. It wasn't that she did anything particularly special; she just did what she was supposed to do.

I took about six or seven teachers from Hardy. JPS was closing Forest Hill Junior High, and Siwell was replacing it and merging with Westside, so I took some teachers from Forest Hill, too.

I had to have good people at Siwell to make it work because we were merging two different communities. I knew I'd have to have some broadminded people in order for it to work. They needed to understand my philosophy, and Jane understood mine, but she was more than just that.

THE CHEERLEADER SAGA AT SIWELL

The spring of my first year at Siwell, I had to elect cheerleaders. I tried to be fair. I wanted to make sure we had some minority cheerleaders on the squad. We had some parents who didn't think that was right because their kids weren't elected. There were five parents, all white, who came into my office. They were PTA members. They said the kids wanted so-and-so on the cheerleading squad and that was who it ought to be. I explained to them that this school would be a little bit different. I knew that we had to represent everyone that went to Siwell. It didn't make sense to have black kids on the football team, but not have any black cheerleaders. We needed black cheerleaders. The parents didn't like that explanation, so they went straight to Dr. Fortenberry. He supported me on my decision. We had practiced this process at Hardy when the school was thirty-five percent white. I was just doing what I normally did and what I thought was fair for all. I weathered that storm. Ninety percent of superintendents would have been swayed by the parents. Not Dr. Fortenberry. That was part of the reason I ended up being a deputy superintendent. Dr. Fortenberry agreed with me on the majority of my decisions.

JANE BRYAN: "BEFORE OUR EYES, DR. HAYNES CLEANED IT UP"

Jane Bryan was teaching first grade at West Point when her husband, Charles, took a job in Jackson, so they moved to Jackson. She got a job at Hardy and had a rough beginning.

"It was tough. I went from teaching sweet little first graders to Hardy. I was only there for one year, but it seemed like fifteen. Another principal retired, and we heard about a new principal who had been hired. We heard that he officiated football in the SEC.

"Dr. Haynes was marvelous. Before our eyes, he cleaned it up. He gained the respect of the faculty on opening day. The students learned to respect him. When you told him something, he followed up. There was no question, he had the students' best interest at heart. You could tell the difference the moment you walked through the front door. The students were taught how to use the facilities. The students were told to go into the auditorium. Dr. Haynes got down to the nitty-gritty. Discipline came first.

"Dr. Haynes brought discipline in school-wide. He required you to stand in the doorway. He was everywhere. Dr. Haynes was like the Energizer Bunny. You never knew where he would pop up. When Dr. Haynes gave the students and teachers a job to do, you just did it.

"I taught individual learning and reading. The students would go at their own pace. Once they met the criteria, they would go to the next step. When Dr. Haynes came into the classroom, he knew what was going on. He took an interest in the kids. They had a goal, an objective every day. They improved academically, and we were proud of them. We saw how much they accomplished and how they turned things around. Dr. Haynes showed them personal attention."

CHAPTER SIX

Greenville School District

Gracie Menhel worked as my administrative assistant while I was the superintendent of the Greenville School District.

"I was so impressed with Dr. Haynes from the beginning," Menhel said. "We were going through some rocky times when Dr. Haynes came. We had our first black superintendent from Chicago. He cut down our magnolia trees and our pretty azalea bushes. He also fired the white people in the administrative offices. After the school district had had enough of him, they fired him. Arthur Payton, a black man, and Janice Ferguson, a white woman, took over and put the district back together. They did a great job. I loved working there; it was my life, other than my family. I decided that I wanted my job back and called Mr. Payton. He wanted to know why I hadn't called sooner. I returned the next Monday. Sharon Norris, a black woman, was, also, hired back and had the same position that I had. We were the same across the board. When Dr. Haynes was hired, it was totally unexpected. We thought Mr. Payton was going to get the job. But Dr. Haynes was so charismatic and captivating. It was like we had a movie star in our midst. He was so kind to us. He told us that we had a good education system in place and that he wasn't going to change anything. I had graduated from that system, and I knew that we had a good reputation. Dr. Haynes was going to lean heavily on our positions. He came to us in his own glory, and he had plenty to be proud about. But he was humble and never boasted. He recognized that we once were the literary capital. We were amazed at the number of people he knew. The number of people he knew could have earned him a spot in *The Guinness Book of World Records*. He asked people to help fund the Mississippi Delta. He wanted to send the band — the Black and Gold Solid Gold Band — to the Rose Bowl.

"We saw them off at midnight, and Dr. Haynes got us to write letters to a lot of people to help pay for the trip. He wasn't bashful at all about asking for money. And one of the first things he did was put our district in uniforms. There was some opposition to it, but Dr. Haynes didn't back down from it. It certainly helped the children and parents financially. It also gave the churches and civic groups a way to sponsor the kids, and it helped them buy their uniforms. I remember seeing Dr. Haynes walking down the hall. He had a kid by his belt. His feet were hardly touching the ground. Dr. Haynes told him that he did not want his pants to sag.

"Dr. Haynes would stop on Alexander Street and stop the school car even though the street was busy. He wasn't bashful about doing the right thing.

"Dr. Haynes told me some of the dearest stories, and they have stuck with me. One of them was about a boy who was a student when Dr. Haynes was a principal in Jackson. He would carry his schedule in his shirt pocket. That story is an inspiration to me.

"I watched Dr. Haynes do some great things with our district. We had some troublesome students. The principal would constantly send one of them to us because he would get into trouble, and Dr. Haynes would send him back to the principal. One of Dr. Haynes' sayings was 'We are not here to put kids out of school, we are here to keep kids *in* school.'

"I retired when Dr. Haynes left. It was one of the saddest days of my life. For the past seven years, I have worked with the detention center, keeping records.

"When Dr. Haynes was scouting referees, he would ask me to type up his reports for his games. Mr. Leo Miles, the supervisor of the recruitment department in the NFL, would call me Miss Gracie, Southern Belle, and the Mouth of the South. I never got a chance to meet him.

"Dr. Haynes has a lovely wife and children. He always made me feel like a part of their family.

"He also told me 'to be very careful who you get your picture taken with' because if you do, ten years from now, that person might not be the same person you knew when you had your picture taken with them."

THE RUSSIAN CONNECTION

I went to Russia in February of 1997 on a student exchange program. One of the teachers I met was Suetlama Akimova. We called her Lama. I visited her class in Russia. Lama decided to come over to the United States as an exchange teacher and spent four months in Greenville. She came back two years later and taught English, Russian, and German.

Lama is an extremely grateful immigrant. She came as a chaperone and liked what she saw. Senator Trent Lott helped us get her green card and citizenship, and I pointed out how important she was to our district. She could teach three foreign languages and could speak English better than some native speakers could. Lama was a gold mine.

"I was excited to have the opportunity to see the United States firsthand and learn more about the country and its people," Lama said. "Dr. Haynes desired for me to stay here and helped get the paperwork done for me to stay. My husband, Ivan Sr., and son, Ivan Jr., moved here, too. This is my eleventh year in Greenville. There have been several superintendents after him, but he was the best. Since the first time I saw him, he was very friendly. Dr. Haynes made a great impression on me. Even though he didn't speak Russian when he came to Russia, I felt comfortable around him. Even though he was a high ranking administrator, he showed interest in every person. An example of his caring personality was that he wrote me a very nice letter, complementing me on receiving an award. It was greatly appreciated, and it made me feel very good and appreciated."

CHAPTER SEVEN

Institutions of Higher Learning Events

(IHL)

I didn't know that being a College Board member (1987-1992) was a big honor until I got on the board. Governor Ray Mabus was the governor during that time.

Mr. George Washington left the board because he was appointed to the public service commission. Alcorn State's national alumni president, Mr. Matt Thomas, called me in the spring of 1987 and said they needed to get another Alcornite on the board to replace George Washington and that my name had popped up. Matt went to Governor Ray Mabus, and Governor Mabus called and interviewed me. I carried a résumé down there and talked to him. My appointment went to the senate and confirmation committee, and they asked me a lot of questions. About four weeks later, I received a call from the governor, and he said I was confirmed. Mr. George Washington was the vice-president, so I became vice-president.

"I worked hard to help get Governor Mabus elected, and he made a promise that he would make appointments to the board and make good representation when the opportunity presented itself," Matt Thomas said. "I thought Joe would make a great representative for several reasons. He had experience with education and working with the secondary schools, which are feeders into college. Joe also fulfilled avenues because he was a man of integrity, and he has excellent moral conduct coming from the African-American community. And he was an Alcorn alumnus, but he represented all eight universities and had a vast knowledge of them.

"I was the national alumni president of Alcorn then, and I ran Joe's name by several individuals within the Alcorn family, but also with alumni from other schools and everyone was for Joe's nomination. It wasn't just Matt Thomas doing this; there were many individuals who believed Joe was the right man for this position, and the rest is history. Joe did a very good job on the College Board."

"I nominated Dr. Haynes based on the recommendations of a number of people whom I trusted and respected, all of whom spoke very highly of the quality of Dr. Haynes' work and the depth of his commitment to public education," Gov. Mabus said. "Dr. Haynes and I had actually met prior to the interview for the board nomination. Before, during, and after that interview, I was always impressed by Dr. Haynes' demeanor, dedication, and preparation. What struck me during my interview with him for the board nomination was how much Dr. Haynes had thought about the issues facing the university system and how measured and thoughtful he was in his analysis of possible solutions.

"I believe Dr. Haynes added a unique perspective to the board. He made it better in multiple ways, including his always calm and courteous demeanor, his exceptional preparation, and his well thought-out solutions to the challenges facing the board. I think Dr. Haynes' most obvious traits are his thoughtfulness, his measured approach, his consistent and exceptional preparation, and his courteousness.

"Perhaps the most important of Dr. Haynes' attributes is that he, obviously, not only learned from his own experiences, but continually brought those lessons into play. His career demonstrates the depth of his commitment to future generations. He is one of the most dedicated and finest individuals I have ever had the privilege to know."

"Joe was a prominent athlete in college and had a good reputation as a referee and did an excellent job on the College Board," said Dr. Ray Cleere, who served as commissioner of the College Board while Dr. Haynes was on it. "We had the Ayers case staring us in the face, getting more resources for African American schools and possibly doing away with some African American schools. We had a mainstreamer like Joe, and he did things for Mississippi and was on the fair side of things."

"I found Joe to be committed to the job," said Dr. Ann Homer Cook, who was the associate commissioner for the IHL, while Dr. Haynes was on the board. "It is difficult to balance the interests of eight public universities. Joe worked hard to do that. You have to put aside your individual loyalties and do what is good for the system. Joe was on the board during a difficult time during the Ayers case. Joe diligently tried to find closure in the Ayers case. He tried to find equality, but he was also aware of the impact on history."

The Ayers case started in 1975 when Jake Ayers Sr. filed suit on behalf of his children and other black college students. It ended in 2004 when the U.S. Supreme Court refused to hear an appeal of the lawsuit, stopping the three-decade battle over state support of the three historically black universities. The state agreed in 2002 to a settlement that would distribute $503 million over seventeen years. This settlement was designed to correct the past neglect of Jackson State, Mississippi Valley State, and Alcorn State universities.

"I knew of Joe Haynes before I ever met him. He was on the College Board before I became chancellor at Ole Miss," said Dr. Robert Khayat, who served as chancellor at Ole Miss while Joe was on the board. "People in higher education talk to each other, and, without exception, Joe Haynes is very well thought of. He is a good listener; he is thoughtful, fair, and doesn't let race be an issue. He has served effectively and well.

"Joe is one of those people who have a rare passion for service. He has a knack for bringing people together for one goal or one cause. Joe has compassion for other people. He is comfortable in any setting, whether it be economical or political differences between people. He has inspired and challenged the black community, and they should model themselves after him. Joe is like a Trojan, and he works extremely hard at whatever he is into. I have great admiration, affection, and respect for Joe. He sees a problem as an opportunity. Joe is in a group of people who rise above the disagreements, misunderstandings, and misdeeds of the past and looks forward to the future."

"Joe is a very likable person. It was always a pleasure to talk to Joe and his wife Dorothy at the education meetings," said Dr. Aubrey Lucas, who was president of the University of Southern Mississippi from 1975-1997, the last two periods he served as the interim president from 2001-2002 and 2012-2013. "It gave him a good idea what our work was all about. Joe had been in administration in the Jackson Public Schools. He knew what we were talking about because his work was like ours. Joe was non-partisan. He didn't favor his alma mater or any other institution. Joe wanted to do what was best for all institutions. He was a careful listener. When I needed to talk to him, I got his ear, and he paid attention to what I had to say. I always trusted Joe with making good decisions, and he never disappointed me."

"Joe was very supportive of Alcorn when he was on the College Board. He helped Alcorn and was interested in our school when we weren't treated fairly," said Dr. Rudolph Waters, who was at Alcorn from 1957-2005 and held many positions in administration, mostly executive vice-president. "Joe knew our mission at Alcorn and didn't want anyone tinkering with that mission.

"I first met Joe when he was a student at Alcorn. He was a good student, a physical education major. I know he also was a football official and was very good in his field. He has done some outstanding things in administration. Joe gets along well with people. He is honest and supports his family well."

"Dr. Haynes understood the issues and had a good grasp of the education system from K-12 and, also, in higher education," said Dr. Cassie Pennington, who lives in Indianola and was on the College Board from 1989-2000. "Joe is well-rounded and has a solid background. He has been an NFL referee, a coach, a player, an assistant principal and assistant superintendent. Dr. Haynes and I have a lot of similarities because I have been a teacher, principal, assistant superintendent, and a college football and basketball official. He knows how to deal with people. Small things can broaden your knowledge of the issues. Dr. Haynes has grass roots knowledge. He has gone from the bottom to the top."

One of the most important decisions I made while I was on the College Board was when I was vice-president in 1990 and we passed a motion to recognize Martin Luther King Jr. Day as a holiday for the universities and colleges in the state.

On this particular board meeting day, Mr. Will Hickman was the president, and he wasn't present. I didn't think there would be any opposition among the people. It was just something we hadn't addressed. Ole Miss, Mississippi State, and Southern Miss were out because of the Robert E. Lee holiday. Jackson State, Alcorn, and Mississippi Valley State were out because it was a holiday. I caught Dr. Cleere off guard when I said that we needed to add something new to the agenda across the system (Martin Luther King Jr. holiday). It sort of unnerved him a little bit, but he said, "Okay, fine." Here I was asking for something that seemed like we had skirted or skipped it, but it was an issue that was important to the College Board. It probably wouldn't have ever gotten on the agenda if I hadn't done anything that day. So, we got it on the agenda. Ann Cook was a very helpful associate commissioner. We had a somewhat controversial thing. We put it up for a vote. We had enough votes on the board that day to get the proposal passed.

We were at the Mississippi University of Women for our next board meeting. For a resolution to pass, it has to be voted on a second time. White supremist, Richard Barrett, heard that the board was about to make it a Martin Luther King Jr. holiday. Richard Barrett came up and talked about why it shouldn't be a holiday. All the board members voted for the holiday after Richard Barrett ranted and raved against the holiday. It wasn't even a discussion. Nobody wanted to take Richard Barrett's position. That said something about the interworking of the board. We allowed him to talk and have his say. That's the democratic way. But his opinion was so far out in left field that no one wanted to be associated with him.

Will Hickman taught me a lot when he was president and I was vice-president. One Wednesday evening, the night before the Thursday's board meeting, Will Hickman was upset because I had added the Martin Luther King Jr. holiday in his absence as I was the vice-president. He berated me and said it was unprofessional of me, I shouldn't have done that, and that I knew better. He went on and on. He put the lawyer stuff to me big time.

I said, "Will, you were not present, and it wasn't a negative thing. I wasn't trying to instigate any riots or anything; I was just trying to get this on the agenda."

He thought I'd taken advantage of the situation.

This is the greatest group of people you ever wanted to be around. There were so many great educators on the board. I learned so much about people and human nature that was beneficial. I don't know how I didn't go crazy then because I was deputy superintendent of Jackson Public Schools and an NFL referee in the United States and in Europe. I was busy. I was on all kinds of committees. It was a full-time job almost. I learned to delegate. There was a time when people were trying to make all the colleges play each other or to force Ole Miss and Mississippi State to play Southern Mississippi, but we didn't want to get into all of that. We wanted the leaders of the universities to do that.

One of my most memorable events as a member of the State College Board came on May 13, 1989, when former President George H. Bush Sr. came to Alcorn State to deliver the commencement ceremony. Alcorn has a great tradition, and the president of the United States' visit added to its rich heritage and tradition. All of the IHL board members attended this ceremony. Normally, only some of the IHL board members would come to a university's ceremony, but never all of them. Dr. Walter Washington was very instrumental in getting the president to speak at the ceremony. President Bush also spoke at Mississippi State that day. This event was a major highlight because I am a proud graduate of Alcorn, and having someone that important come to my school made me very proud of our university. My wife, Dorothy, had a chance to meet the president and members of his entourage. It was also one of her most memorable events, and we often talk about it. She is an Alcorn graduate, as well.

This was my first real live opportunity to see the president of the United States and how much security surrounded him at an event. Security surrounded the campus, and everyone on the State College Board had to submit information several weeks ahead of time because we were going to be on the stage with the president. Security was very tight. We had to get there an hour before the president's arrival, and there was a huge amount of security surrounding the stage and campus. We flew to Alcorn and landed in Natchez and drove from Natchez to the campus in a motorcade.

President Bush came by helicopter to the campus. We also left Lorman and went to Mississippi State for its ceremony that afternoon. Although the president came in on a helicopter, the press plane flew to Natchez. Then, the press took a motorcade to the campus.

Another highlight of my tenure on the State College Board was when my wife and I attended an event where U.S. Senator John Stennis of Mississippi was honored in Washington D.C. and President Ronald Reagan was one of the speakers.

The following is a small group of people who were extremely influential during my time with the State College Board:

WALTER WASHINGTON (president of Alcorn State from 1969-94)

In my opinion, Walter Washington was the best president Alcorn has ever had. When I was on the State College Board, I was on the building committee. I had that experience because, when I was deputy superintendent of Jackson Public Schools, I dealt with the buildings and maintenance. While on the building committee, I questioned part of a contract for a building for Alcorn. No one expected me, being an Alcornite, to question it, but I did.

The next week, I got a visit from Dr. Waters, the assistant at Alcorn, and he asked me if there was anything they could do to satisfy me. I had ruffled Dr. Washington's feathers, and he sent Dr. Waters to make sure I was okay.

Another time, I made a casual trip to Alcorn when my son was a student there to take him some money. I was on the State College Board at the time, and you couldn't just go onto a college campus without letting them know. Some of the security saw me on campus and told Dr. Washington. He had them come get me and take me to his office. He didn't appreciate me coming to his campus without letting him know. He was in charge. I learned about being on the board from Dr. Washington. I respected his leadership. In October 2011, I was able to attend a dedication ceremony for a highway in his name that leads to the campus at Lorman.

DR. AUBREY LUCAS (president of University of Southern Mississippi from 1975-1997, the last two periods he served as the interim president from 2001-2002 and 2012-2013)

Dr. Lucas would never let you get comfortable as a board member. He always had a good joke to tell. He is very personable. If the board was uptight about some issue, he would tell a story, and everyone would laugh. Dr. Lucas wore a bow tie. He is a great guy, and he always talked to us even when the board was not in session. I have a tremendous amount of respect for Dr. Lucas. When I had a fundraising event for Jobs for Mississippi Graduates in Hattiesburg in 2010, I invited him to come, and out of respect for me, he came. I know he didn't have time because he has a very busy schedule, but he was there. Dr. Lucas is a rock. He did a wonderful job as the president of Southern Mississippi.

DR. ROBERT KHAYAT (Chancellor at University of Mississippi from 1995-2009)

Dr. Khayat worked for the NCAA before he became dean of the law school at Ole Miss. Dr. Khayat had a brother who was an assistant coach for the New England Patriots, and we would always talk about things when I was an official in the NFL. Whenever Dr. Khayat and I got together, we could relate about Kansas City because I was on the governing board of the national high school federation, and he worked for the NCAA. Even before he was chancellor, he had the talent to bring people together. We got to know each other when he was the dean of the law school and then when he became chancellor. I was on the State College Board, and it was very easy to talk to him about matters of Ole Miss and the State College Board because we already had a great relationship. He was the kind of guy who was never intrusive, he was never pushy, and he was always a team player. You could tell he had played sports and had vast experiences that made him a leader.

DR. LOUISE JONES (education leadership professor at Jackson State from 1977 to 2002)

The reason she stands out is because, when I left Jackson Public Schools, I was very bitter. I had been passed over for the superintendent's job after being the deputy under Dr. Robert Fortenberry. After two or three years, I got a payoff from JPS, and I was looking for a job. I talked to Dr. Lyons. At that time, he was the president of Jackson State, and I told him I needed a job. They had a vacancy in leadership, where they trained principals and educators. They gave me the acting position.

Dr. Jones had been the chairperson of that department. We had a lot of national teacher certification studies, too, and there were several tenured professors who needed to support the work effort. I had the ability to be the leader, and Dr. Jones had the ability to do the work. She unselfishly said she would help me. Dr. Jones is a magnificent person. She helped me do all of the little things I had to do to be a department chair on a college campus. Because of her help, I was named the Department Chairperson of the Year at Jackson State.

DR. DONALD ZACHARIUS (president of Mississippi State University from 1985 to 1997)

Dr. Zacharias and his wife did a tremendous job for Mississippi State while he was president. He was the epitome of leadership. He was very professional. When Mississippi State went to the College World Series in Omaha, all of the State College Board members went. I never will forget that experience. We had dinner at a barbeque place in Omaha, and Dr. Zacharias went out of his way to make sure my wife and I felt very comfortable there. I have a baseball with Ron Polk's and Dr. Zacharias' autograph. He was a first-class leader in Mississippi. Dr. Zacharias was very genuine, and he would always make me feel comfortable when I visited Mississippi State's campus. I was in the first class of graduate fellows from Mississippi State, and I am positive that Dr. Zacharius was instrumental in my achievement of that status.

DR. GERALD TURNER (Chancellor at Ole Miss from 1984 to 1995)

He was the chancellor at Ole Miss. In my opinion, Gerald Turner changed my whole attitude about Ole Miss. He was a very nice guy. Gerald was a lay minister. He can take basic concepts and turn them into a powerful speech. I have some of his outlines. For example, the subject of character. He would have four or five little things and make a great speech on character.

He invited my wife and me to the Ole Miss campus, and we spent the night at his house. I was dealing with the James Meredith days, and you can never hide the history, but Gerald Turner made us feel so welcome. We spent the night at his house, and had breakfast at his house. I remember that. That was a gesture that was beyond the call of duty. Gerald Turner was such a warm guy. He was a great influence in my life.

DR. ANN HOMER COOK (Associate commissioner of the State College Board from 1986 to 1994)

Dr. Cook was the associate commissioner under Dr. Ray Cleere. She kept me straight. I was vice-chairman and chairman while I was on the State College Board. I will never forget the many times that Dr. Cook helped me out. During the controversial voting to pass the Martin Luther King holiday for the universities, Dr. Cook communicated to me that I better count the votes.

She meant, I had it won, so don't lose it. So, we called for a vote. We had enough votes for the resolution to pass. Dr. Cook was the proponent of that. If I had just sat around and continued to talk about it and let people discuss it further, we might not have gotten the resolution to pass.

GOVERNOR RAY MABUS (Governor of Mississippi from 1988-1992 and Secretary of the Navy from 2004-present)

You have to be vetted before you can be approved by the peer committee to serve on the State College Board. Governor Ray Mabus wanted me to come to his office for an interview. I could tell he had done his homework. He knew everything was okay. It was just a matter of him looking at me face-to-face and talking. He talked about my ability to make decisions and asked me questions about my decision-making. He wanted to know if I could be independent and that was it. I thought it was going to be a long interview, but I wasn't in there any longer than ten minutes.

After I was appointed, I had to be confirmed by the Senate. The peer committee had done their homework, and they had related it to the governor. He just had to meet me face-to-face. Governor Mabus was easygoing and had the people of the state at heart. He was a humanitarian. He has proven that because he is now the secretary of the Navy. Governor Mabus is very approachable.

DR. JOE BLACKBOURN SR. (A professor in the Department of Education Leadership at Mississippi State University from 1968-1999)

Dr. Blackbourn was my advisor while I completed my doctoral work at Mississippi State. I will never forget him because I was kind of hesitant about going into a doctoral program. I didn't want to start without finishing. That was a big step. While we were working out my schedule, Dr. Blackbourn suggested that I take the tough courses early because, he said, if I did not finish statistics and the other hard courses, I wasn't going to graduate anyway. He kind of scared me, but he also directed me toward the right path. He is one of my favorite people.

When I wrote my dissertation, Dr. Blackbourn was on the committee. They had written all over it. I turned it back in and corrected it three or four times. Right in the middle of that, a new dean was hired. The new dean took a look at it and made a lot of corrections, too. So, I had to redo it. The committee had approved it previously before the new dean had looked at it, and Dr. Blackbourn was the head of the committee. He said I didn't have to correct it again, but my whole philosophy in life was "I didn't want any problems", and I didn't want to graduate if the new dean wasn't satisfied with my dissertation.

DR. WILLIAM SUTTON (Mississippi Valley State from 1988-1998)

Dr. Sutton was an excellent president at Valley during the period of time when there were a lot of questions about closing the university. He was steadfast that the university's mission was kept intact. Dr. Sutton was keenly aware that Valley had a purpose when it was originally founded — to educate poor minority kids in the Mississippi Delta. When the issue came up of Delta State and Valley State merging, Dr. Sutton was instrumental in making sure that both universities maintained their individual identities. Dr. Sutton's stance on maintaining the mission at Valley State was controversial, to say the least. However, his ideas prevailed, and contrary to the opinion of some board members that he should be terminated, he survived and retired gracefully. Thanks to his persistence, Valley State is still a viable part of the university system and is serving its mission as of this writing. Valley State is fulfilling its mission despite some of the pitfalls that surround all of the universities in the state of Mississippi, such as funding.

DR. TOM MEREDITH

Dr. Meredith is a longtime IHL administrator/teacher that made an excellent impression on my career as I was getting ready to pursue a master's degree at the University of Georgia in 1969. I was able to take some courses to transfer from the Mississippi universities as part of my master's program, and Dr. Meredith taught a class in public relations in administration that inspired me greatly. Dr. Meredith went on to be the IHL commissioner in Mississippi. He was also a college administrator for several years. He had a wealth of knowledge about higher education systems.

CHAPTER EIGHT

At the University of Georgia

(Life Changing Events)

I choose to attend the University of Georgia in 1969 for post-graduate studies for two reasons—one, because a degree from a black college, like Alcorn State, wasn't recognized as having a quality education, and, two, because the state department of education would pay for an out-of-state degree if it wasn't offered at an in-state school. I had a scholarship from the American Association of Traffic Safety.

When I went to Georgia, I met a guy named Eddie Stone who has had a great impact on my life. I was one of the few black students on the large campus — an estimated enrollment of 21,000 at the time.

Eddie was very different from me. He was white; I was black. He was from Georgia. I was from Mississippi. He had a fastback Mustang. I had an old Chevy. We were assigned as roommates. Even though we were very different, we got along great.

"I had gotten to Morris Hall, checked in, and gotten my room assignment. I remember asking the person who was assigning the rooms if I had a roommate," Eddie said. "His name is Joe Haynes from Jackson, Mississippi. The first thing that went through my mind was, 'That's a good ole redneck boy from Mississippi. We're going to get along fine.' I went up to my room, went out, got dinner, and came back, no roommate. I picked out which bed I wanted, and he hadn't shown up. It got on up to ten o'clock, eleven o'clock, and I said, 'Well, I'm going to go ahead and go to bed.' I didn't figure Joe was coming.

"About three o'clock in the morning, I woke up. The door slammed open, and he flipped on the lights, carrying a bunch of bags. I rolled over and sat up. At that time, he was the biggest black guy I had ever seen in my life. He was big, muscular, and solid as a rock. He had big neck muscles. And I thought, 'Lord, what is happening here?' He came in and said he was Joe Haynes. I got out of my bed in my underwear and told him who I was. I thought, 'I just don't know about this.' I had never been around any black people. Being from the real segregated South, from Newnan, Georgia, I didn't have any reference points. Joe went to bed pretty quick. He was tired."

"I didn't give it a whole lot of thought after Joe got there. I went back to bed," Eddie said. "I woke up the next morning, and Joe was still asleep. I thought I would go get some breakfast. Joe rolled around and woke up and asked me where I was going. He wanted to go with me because he was hungry. He said he had eaten in Alabama on his way over here and was really hungry. He had gotten turned around in Atlanta and lost some time, so he didn't stop to get anything. I said, 'Sure, you can go with me.' We got in my car, got acquainted over breakfast, and talked about what we had to do. We went to register. I knew where to go, and Joe talked about how fast registration was. We had a class together. We went back after registration and had dinner together. I had a 1966 Mustang Hatchback. It was a hot car. I don't ever remember going anywhere in Joe's car, he had a Chevy II. We hit it off and did everything together."

This situation had a profound effect on me. I had a different idea about why I was there. I was there to make a point. After I got there, things started clicking. The whole staff was very receptive, and my whole attitude was different. Eddie was great, and we would talk about things late into the night. It gave me a different perspective. You've got to remember, I went to Alcorn, and we had an archaic registration system. It would probably take two or three days to get my class schedule.

"I can't explain why I didn't see Joe as a black guy," Eddie said. "Maybe, it was Joe's personality. I had gone through undergraduate work at West Georgia College, and I didn't see any black kids there, and our high schools in Newnan were totally segregated. Other than the black kids I played with in summer baseball, I didn't have any interaction with black people. I had a great relationship with the black kids who I played baseball with, though. Almost none of the black kids had gloves, and we would give them our gloves when we came to the bat. I noticed that the black kids acted like different people when they would play against other black kids. They were more aggressive—sliding into bases, rolling people over at home. We couldn't believe it. I wondered if they didn't want to be super aggressive with us white guys because we were friends. I felt bad because they didn't feel they could be themselves around us and felt they had to be more docile around us."

Let me try to put that into perspective. I don't totally know the situation, but you could imagine what it must have been like to be a minority. We had a mindset that was different. From my perspective, I was not supposed to be here, and I did not want to offend anyone. I wanted to do the right thing, so it was easy to be in an easy mode. I wanted to be accepted.

I was the only black person in a class of thirty-six at the University of Georgia, so most probably thought they were smarter than I was. Eddie and I had a management class together, and we were studying the night before the test. All of a sudden, Eddie just threw the book across the room and said, "I'm going to get a good night's sleep and go over it in the morning."

I had immense pressure on me to do well on this test and here Eddie was not studying any more for the rest of the night. I felt I had to make up for my so-called deficiencies since I was from a black college in Mississippi, so I thought I had to study longer and harder than Eddie.

We took the test, and the teacher said he would write the As and Bs on the board and throw the Cs, Ds, and Fs in the garbage. He wrote Eddie's name and a ninety-seven beside it, and I started sweating. I thought, What if I don't do well on this test, while my roommate made a ninety-seven? What then? The teacher then wrote my name on the board and a ninety-six beside it. I was very excited. I felt confident, then, in my abilities. As a result of that grade, people came up to me and wanted to know how I studied and if I could study with them.

Out of all the classmates I had, Eddie Stone is the only person I can visualize now after forty odd years. I could never have had a finer roommate. He was such a nice guy. If there was anything wrong with Eddie, as far as race was concerned, he never showed it. That's why it was so easy for us to get along. We used to ride together, go to movies together, and hang out together. My relationship with Eddie and going to the University of Georgia made me think that I could be an SEC official, made me think that I could get a doctorate degree, made me think I could be an NFL official. It is amazing how that one encounter affected me. I had so much self-confidence after that. I believed I could do anything. It relieved me of an anxiety and pressure that was engrained.

"Joe is easy to talk to, very forthcoming, never in your face about anything, very casual in his demeanor, and a very genuine person. I felt that from the first morning I met him," Eddie said. "I felt comfortable around him. You don't want to be around someone you aren't comfortable with. Life is too short for that, but I felt good around Joe. That's my basic style, too. I'm pretty even-keeled. The highs are never too high, and the lows are never too low. That's just the way I am. I get disappointed; I get hurt, but I don't let it bother me.

"I'm as Southern as I can be. I saw that segregation was going on, but I thought that was the way people wanted it to be. I judged a lot of people against the standards that I saw in Joe. I'm sorry to say that Joe set a standard in my eyes that not many have lived up to. It showed me that there are people of all races that are just like me. I am a better person for being good friends with Joe. I feel more comfortable in my own skin.

"I was impressed with Joe being a married person. Most of the people were married when we were in graduate school, but I wasn't married at the time and never thought I would be because all this stuff about love and commitment was a bunch of bull. When I saw Joe, I saw that marriage and love was real. Joe was dedicated to his wife and his family, and it was extremely hard for him to be away. He called his wife every night and talked to her. I thought, they must be good friends, too. I came away from all that believing that your wife has got to be your best friend, too. I appreciated that in him. I was a pretty cynical person about marriage and commitment and all that. It wasn't about Joe. I automatically think about the negatives about things, but Joe made me think differently. I got married about a year later. I traded my Mustang — and I loved my Mustang more than anything in this world — for a '62 Volkswagen and $1,000 in cash to buy an engagement ring. I was committing right there, wasn't I? I sent Joe an invitation to my wedding. It's not like I didn't want Joe to come, but I didn't think he would. I would have been happy for Joe to be there. I felt strongly enough about Joe, and I wanted to send him an invitation. It wouldn't have been uncomfortable for me if Joe had been there."

We had talked about things, Eddie's life and my life. When Eddie sent that wedding invitation to me, it all started coming together. He had sent the invitation because he wanted me to know. I was Eddie's best friend, but I was not going to go to Newnan, Georgia, to a wedding out of protection for him. I wanted to meet his bride and his family, but I didn't want to make him feel uncomfortable. I felt that, if I went to the wedding, I would.

I graduated in the top ten percent of my class. I didn't go to graduation because I had to get back to Mississippi and help out my wife with our baby son.

Going to the University of Georgia and rooming with Eddie taught me that I could be judged on my ability instead of my color, and it also gave me the confidence that I had a good head on my shoulders. The management class that I took helped produce my administrative style, but the relationship I had with Eddie Stone changed my life forever.

CHAPTER NINE

Jobs for Mississippi Graduates

I was sitting at the state department of education in a staff meeting one day. I was one of the staffers for Dr. Richard Thompson, the state superintendent of education, back in 2000. I'd had the opportunity to look at this curriculum at Jobs for Mississippi Graduates when I was the superintendent in Greenville. This program was exactly what we needed. We had students who were lacking in the ninth grade and were about to drop out of school and be on the streets. They needed guidance. I learned about it then. So, JMG had a vacancy. The program had financial problems. It was a private non-profit. Dr. Thompson said the job only paid $57,000, but it wasn't about the money. I believed I could make a difference, so I applied for the job and got it.

JMG is the kind of work I love. I have worked for forty years, more or less, in education. But JMG has been a little bit different. It is about somebody taking people who are kind of loose, about to fall off the page, and working with them and seeing them grow and do well. Everything about this can be applied to officiating, to any kind of leadership position, to an administrator in a school where students are. My greatest success was when I was an assistant principal a long time ago. I utilized many methods to get students to change their behavior. I would say, "Hey, look. I got you."

They would say, "Yeah, you got me."

I would take that opportunity and say, "Look. Let's forget this. Let's not dwell on this. Just don't do it again. I'm going to let you off. I got you. I could send you home. I could paddle you. I could do all those things."

But I would use that opportunity to talk to them. Most of the time, they would get better. That will happen in all walks of life, even in this organization. Even with teachers. If our teachers failed to do what they were supposed to do, I would call them in and talk to them. They would get better, not worse. It was that conversation piece. It's the fact you are giving them a second chance. I was treating them like people. I respected them, and I valued them as human beings. I have found this true in officiating and in education.

In my years of officiating, I found that people with that kind of attitude improved people and made them better. Those that didn't have that kind of attitude, I would tell them to get out of here. Just as fast as I did that, it would be like starting over again. If I didn't, I knew I would never get a chance to capture the leadership, the growth the person had, or the investment I'd made in that person.

We have kids that nobody would have predicted to be successful. But we gave them a second chance. I enjoy this work. You give me forty-five students who don't believe in anything, and we will give them back to you next year ready to conquer the world. It's not rocket science. It's all about counseling and giving them support. It's about finding out what they need to understand what life is all about.

We have been growing since I took over. We are doing well, even in a tight economy. We know, for a fact, we can make a difference. Every person that works in this organization has empathy for these kids. We have fifty-five schools across the state. We have hired the very best counselors to help these kids that might have very little parenting at home. There are a lot of kids who have had kids. Unless we can get to these kids and change their attitude about going to school, we will have another generation like this. I'm going to attack it as hard as I can.

We can take potential and make something out of it. It's that one thing that we can do that many schools can't do. We can take a population of kids that have not had many opportunities to do anything. Take them to Washington, DC, take them to the science museum here in Jackson. A lot of these kids have never been outside of their little towns. These kids can get to see NASA and Nissan. They recognize that they have to study to be proficient in what they are doing. All of a sudden, they see it. If they're going to be a doctor, a lawyer, a sportswriter, they've got to go to school and learn how to do it. They are exposed to things they have never been exposed to. We take them to the Mississippi Department of Transportation (MDOT) plant. They see these different jobs, where all they have to do is push buttons, and they see that they can make twenty-five dollars an hour. A lot of these kids think they have to go to college in order to get a good job.

Out of all of the work I've done during my career, JMG was the one thing that caused my whole life to make a complete circle because of its redemptive power. It is a program that has helped so many young people that were basically lost. We helped them to find jobs and gave them hope. JMG is almost like a ministry. It has led me to do more mentoring work; it has led me to recognize that I cannot give up on kids because they have so much to offer. It works. It improved my faith in humanity by one hundred percent. Even though I had been an NFL official, worked on the State College Board, been a principal and a superintendent, the most satisfying thing in my career has been working with JMG and helping these young people succeed. I was able to see why education was important to young people. I saw situations where a student with little to no parenting was— thanks to the JMG staff— helped, where many other problems were solved, and where they learned to work on a student-to-student basis.

When we first started the program, we had trouble hiring good teachers. My wife, Dorothy, was the teacher at the school. We had a kid at Lanier High School who was living in his car on Bailey Avenue because, when his brother got married, he didn't want to stay at his house. He didn't have any way to get to school and didn't have any lunch. My wife recognized this was a student who needed help. He was eligible to get a ride to school and was also eligible to get a free lunch. He didn't have a mom or dad to fill out any paperwork on him, so my wife decided to go to the different agencies within the school district and get that paperwork done for him. Not a person at the school had recognized his talent, but my wife did. He took the ACT test and made a 29 on it.

Dr. Frances Lucas, then the president of Millsaps College, and I were meeting together, and I told her the story about this student. He went into the Army, but she said, whenever he decided to come back, she would give him a full scholarship. This is an example of what JMG does. We can get teachers who have retired, but still have something to offer, and give them a chance to help a significant number of kids.

The following people had significant involvement in my success as the executive director of Jobs for Mississippi Graduates:

MR. KEN SMITH
Ken is the current CEO and president of Jobs for America's Graduates. He has been the force behind an extremely solid program that has gone national and international. Ken's concern for young people dropping out of high school has been paramount. He has demonstrated his ability to help sustain programs in states where the program might have been on life support due to a multitude of issues. Ken single-handedly helped to resurrect the Mississippi program when it was clear that some major changes needed to be done in the areas of finance and leadership.

DR. RICHARD THOMPSON
Dr. Thompson was a former state superintendent of education in Mississippi and a former board member of the Jobs for America's Graduates. He understood the value of the Jobs for Mississippi Graduates program and was very instrumental in reviving the program during the lean years.

MRS. DOROTHY HAYNES

When I first started as the executive director of JMG, I needed seasoned teachers to serve in the program. Dorothy Haynes, my wife, was a retired technology teacher and had invaluable knowledge about leading young people. I called on her for a lot advice, and she responded by accepting a teaching position in the program that led to phenomenal success.

DR. JIM KOENINGER

Jim Koeninger encouraged me and provided me with support to make the program work. In every organization, there are a group of people who make the organization work. His wife, Kern Koeninger, is a supportive person, too. In my opinion, these two people are the glue that holds JAG together. In other words, they do a lot of the grunt work. They organize the meetings and various other duties for JAG. There are many states in the JAG network.

DR. CAROLYN WARNER

She used to be the chief state school officer in Arizona and has been a national board member for JAG for more than thirty years. When she was a superintendent of schools in Arizona, she recognized that she needed to do something different to help her kids. She said she saw the value of this program when she was a superintendent in Arizona. She supports this program and is currently a board member of the national organization.

MRS. MARSHA BARBOUR

The wife of Governor Barbour took a liking to our program and joined our board. She was instrumental in my success with

JMG. She recognized that we have a lot of kids in this state that need the services we provided. Our CEO, Ken Smith, talked to Mrs. Barbour at the National Governor's Conference about how she could be very helpful to us if she joined the board, and she did. She was on so many boards that she really didn't have time to do a lot with all of them, but she would come to our board meetings, and that's how I knew she was extremely interested in our program.

GOVERNOR HALEY BARBOUR

I know Governor Barbour is extremely busy, but he would go out of his way to attend some of our meetings. He would help us. He believes in redemption, and that's why he liked our program because that is what our mission is all about. Governor Barbour will always be one of my friends. He did a tremendous amount for JMG, and he also strongly believed in our program.

MRS. GLORIA JOHNSON

Gloria Johnson works at Entergy and is a board member. She would always look for ways that Entergy can help this program. She recognizes the value of this program.

MRS. ALICE GAULDEN

Alice was at JMG when I got there about ten years ago. She is the only holdover that is still there now. She is a Christian hearted person, and she and her husband do a lot of outreach work. They work with homeless kids. She is also a sincere worker. Alice is not just there for the job. She is truthful and an extremely hard worker.

MR. HOWARD SANDERS

Howard used to be the superintendent of the Hollandale schools. He recognized the value of this program many years ago. This program has been in Mississippi for, at least, twenty years. There was a time when this program was about to die, but Howard was one of the people who kept it alive. Back in 2000, we couldn't even make payroll. Howard was instrumental in helping the program. When I went to my boss, Richard Thompson, and told him I wanted to run JMG and get this job, Howard Sanders was instrumental in me getting the position.

REP. ROBERT CLARK

Robert was a key person. He helped JMG when it was on its last leg. Robert recognized that poor kids needed a second chance, and he recognized that this program provided that. Robert was on the JMG board and kept the superintendent informed on how the program was doing. He became the senator pro tem.

MRS. RUBY DUMAS

Ruby was a staff member of JMG back in 1995. She came to my office when I was superintendent of Greenville schools and told me that JMG was a program that would help a lot of our kids. I listened to her, and I was convinced this program was something we needed in Greenville. She was instrumental in me seeing the value of JMG and how it would help our school system and our kids. She later worked for us as a job specialist in Montgomery County.

MRS. BETTY HAWKINS

Betty was a retired teacher in Indianola. She inspired me because she took her job very personally. She acted as if it was her fault that these kids had not graduated. She was so into it; she would go find them, and they couldn't hide. She was motivated to go the extra mile to make sure these kids would graduate.

Betty won the national competition in math three or four times. She was an exceptional teacher.

MRS. ELLEN STRAHAN

Ellen is the job specialist in George County. George County is ninety-eight percent white. She is such an important person because she dispelled the myth that only black kids need help. We were able, first of all, to convince the board that this program was needed in George County. They said they would try it. Ellen had more than one hundred people lined up wanting to be in her class. She was able to work with those kids and improve them tremendously. She was able to help them, and I am also grateful to her.

REP. CECIL BROWN

Cecil was the chairman of the education committee at one time. Cecil was a Democrat, and Governor Barbour was a Republican, but there was one thing they agreed on — funding JMG. They recognized the value of this program. Governor Barbour had enough money in 2007 to fund the middle school program for ten schools, but the education committee could only fund five. But, since then, Cecil has funded more. The middle school program was funded because, in middle school, kids have a tendency to get off track, make bad decisions, miss school, and participate in the negative things that are detrimental to education. It made a huge difference. In one example, we cut down the amount of times kids were sent to the principal's office for acting up by eighty-five percent across the board in those five schools.

MRS. KELLY RILEY

Kelly Riley was the education support person for Governor Musgrove. She was the person that I went through to get support from the governor. Kelly was aware of what we were doing, and she helped us. I am grateful for her help, and she saw the good in our program.

MRS. KAY VAN SKIVER

Kay was the president of the Road Builders Association and recognized the value of the program and helped us with fundraising. She helped bring in the president of Shell Oil International. Kay was a go-getter on our board. She would come to Washington when we had meetings. She is a big supporter. Kay's husband is on the board now.

MR. CRAIG LERABEE

Craig was the CEO of JMG for Maine. In 2007, we started a secession plan, and we had a retreat in Mississippi. He was the leader of the retreat, and he talked to the board about how we needed to plan about replacements. He showed us the model he had in Maine, and it worked out fine.

SUPREME COURT JUSTICE RANDY PIERCE

When I first met Justice Pierce, he was a legislator and was supportive of the JMG program. Justice Pierce understood the value of what we were doing to help young people graduate from high school and give them a sense of value. Later on, I wanted to place a program in Greene County, and I called on Justice Pierce to assist me in getting that done. I was successful in getting the program in George County with Justice Pierce's help. The program has been successful in George County, and the extra help Justice Pierce has provided in speaking to students at special occasions has been invaluable.

BARRY GLENN

He is the CEO of the Jobs for Virginia Graduates. Formerly an educator, Barry's greatest contribution is his encouragement to me to put my memoir in writing. Barry and I visited with each other during our convention days, and we would share a lot of human interest stories. He wanted me to put all of my experiences in writing, and he would be one of the first to buy a book. Barry also demonstrated great leadership in Virginia for those students who had drop-off tendencies and needed a helping hand to graduate from high school. Barry's lasting contribution will be measured by his support and a no-nonsense direction to improving Jobs for America's Graduates, our parent organization.

REPRESENTATIVE BENNIE THOMPSON,

Was an avid supporter of JMG. He was always open and honest with us when we were seeking funding grants for JMG.

CHAPTER TEN

Some Significant People in Education

I have been in education for more than forty years, and many people have been influential in my life in that field. I have worked as a teacher, coach, assistant principal, principal, deputy superintendent, superintendent, State College Board president, and associate state superintendent. The following people played a significant role in guiding me during my educational journey.

DR. RUEBEN DILWORTH

He is an educator's educator. He understood the importance of being an encouraging educator. Dr. Dilworth was a Jackson Public Schools central office employee before I was. We were neighbors, and we would always talk about things. When I had a chance to go to the central office, he encouraged me and told me some good things. He made me feel comfortable about making the move instead of being apprehensive and nervous. Dr. Dilworth is a warm and knowledgable person, and he got things done. He recommended me to take the job as the transportation director at JPS. He felt I had all of the tools to get the job done.

DR. JOHN JORDAN

Dr. Jordan was my dormitory counselor when I was getting my doctorate at Mississippi State. He was always a fair-minded person. We were in classes together. John was a unique guy. We had a vacancy in the JPS central office for a personnel director. I was deputy superintendent in charge of operations, and Dr. Fortenberry gave me the authority to hire people. John was the principal at Natchez Cathedral High School, and I went down and visited him at his office. He did everything at Cathedral. I told him what I wanted, and he became the personnel director at JPS. He was influential and loyal.

MR. FRED DAVIS

Fred Davis replaced a guy who had been finance director for twenty-plus years. I had to get a finance director when I was deputy superintendent, and I found Fred. Previously, he had been the director of a savings and loan company. I needed someone with an accounting background who could handle the money. He had been an assistant vice-president in Vicksburg. I went to his office in Vicksburg and tried to hire him. When a board member found out about it, they gave him a raise, but he came with me. It was my mission to hire him. We had $25 million in the reserve fund, and we needed someone knowledgeable to handle the money, and Fred did an outstanding job.

DR. HENRRIETTE ALLEN

Her job was, if there was such a thing, chief of staff to Dr. Fortenberry. In other words, she didn't have anyone to report to her. She was the kind of person who would come to you and tell you that she thought Dr. Fortenberry needed this or that. She was that kind of guiding person. She would keep the board policies up to date. Dr. Allen was always a person I respected. When I became the superintendent at Greenville, I paid Dr. Allen to be a consultant to revamp our board policies.

MR. STEVE WILLIAMS

Steve worked at the state department of education (SDE). He was an assistant superintendent, but he was like a chief of staff under several superintendents. Steve was there when I went to the state department under Richard Thompson. He was just the kind of guy who could bring people together. He's my kind of person because he is the kind of guy who I like and admire.

MRS. JUDY RHODES

Judy was quite influential. She was quiet, but she called the shots for the state department of education for many years. When I was an associate superintendent of the state department of education, I knew, if I needed something done, that I better make sure that Judy Rhodes agreed with it. Although she was not the superintendent and was not the person I reported to, she had a lot of influence. She was always very honest with me. I had many divisions that I was in charge of, and I had good people running them, but every once in a while, I would encounter a sticky issue. Once I had a decision in mind, I would run it by Judy. If she said it was okay, I could count on it that it was the right decision. I would go by and talk to Richard Thompson, and he would give the approval to a decision, but the first thing he did was call Judy and ask her opinion.

DR. RICHARD THOMPSON

Richard Thompson was a great manager. When I was the superintendent in Greenville, he arranged several conversations between me and Judy Rhodes on several different occasions. This was mid-August, and school was about to start. Dr. Thompson had just been appointed as superintendent, and they wanted someone to be an assistant superintendent, more or less. I couldn't leave my school district when school was about to start because it would have left the school district in a bind. I had more respect for the school district, so I turned them down.

About three weeks later, I got a call, and they asked me if I could come in December. I said yes, I could, because that would give me time to announce my resignation and clean up my house up there and come to Jackson. He gave me the exact responsibilities I had when I was at Jackson Public Schools. In other words, in order to make me successful, he wanted to put me in positions that I knew how to do. Richard was supportive. He was a no-nonsense type of guy. Richard was on the board for Jobs for Mississippi Graduates. I saw this job opening for them, and I was interested in it. I talked to Richard, and he said it didn't pay much. That wasn't my reason for wanting the job. I knew I could help someone if I got this job. I'm sure Richard helped me to get the job. He got me the interview, and I got the job. Richard knew I didn't like being in a job where I couldn't help anyone, and I was when I was at the state department. In other words, I was helping, but it wasn't hands-on helping.

MR. EDDIE STONE

Eddie Stone was my roommate when we attended the University of Georgia; however, we shared many experiences together. Eddie and I learned a lot from each other, but, more than that, we learned to respect each other. There is a chapter in this book that tells about our unique relationship. We built a bond as strong as brothers. After forty years, we met for the first time to work on this book together, and we were able to remember old times like it was yesterday.

MRS. GRACIE MENHALE

She was my secretary at Greenville. She had been the secretary for several superintendents prior to me at Greenville. When I became superintendent, she thought I was going to oust her. I knew, then, that, if I wanted someone to help me, I needed to call and talk to her and see if she was willing to help me. This goes along with my theory. Here is a lady who knew where all the bones were, what all the issues were and everything, so why would I get a new secretary? She stayed on, and she was a jewel. She was first class. I couldn't have been a good superintendent if it had not been for her.

MRS. HELEN HAMEL

Helen was a secretary at Hardy Middle School. When I got the job, everybody said that I had to get a new secretary. You know how people are. They said she didn't have much personality. I appreciated their input, but I found out for myself. I talked to her, and she served me well. She did such a great job that I hired her when I went to Siwell. And then I took her with me to Jackson Public School's central office. She was one of those people who were loyal and competent, and she did an outstanding job.

DR. OKA DUREN

She was a math teacher at Siwell. When I went to Siwell as principal, everybody was an expert at everything because I had the pick of the school district. Since we were a new school, I picked the best teachers. Oka's children were young; her husband was a minister, and she could never get to school on time. So, I had a rule that everyone had to be signed in by a certain time. I always stood by the door and watched people come in. Oka was always late, but I didn't say anything to her. She always stayed after school to tutor kids who needed help because we had so many kids who were failing algebra. Although Oka was five minutes late in the morning, people wanted to know why I didn't say anything to her and punish her. I wasn't going to punish someone who was giving her time after school. Sometimes, she would stay until four or five o'clock helping kids. She was one of those teachers who gave extra all the time.

MR. LOUIE ODOM

Louie Odom was the principal when I was an assistant principal at Provine. He was also the assistant principal at Brinkley. At that time, I was the chairman of driver's education, and I was in charge of keeping the records and making sure the teachers got reimbursed and various other things. We had about ten driver's education teachers, and I was in charge of the department. We had people like Charlie Allman, Orsmond Jordan, Carol Roulette and Ervin Chancellor, and they all had strong personalities. Mr. Odom told me anyone who could lead them could be an assistant principal. He called my wife, Mrs. Dorothy Haynes, and she directed him to me while I was at the University of Georgia working on my master's degree. He asked me to be his assistant principal at Provine. He wanted someone who could handle the kids, show strong discipline, and gain respect from the students. Louie was very straight laced. He was the person who gave me the opportunity to be an administrator. He had about twenty-five years as an officer in the U.S. Army, reaching as high as a colonel, and had worked in the White House and the Pentagon. Louis recognized my ability to manage people, and he gave me my first chance to be an administrator.

DR. ANDY MULLINS
Dr. Mullins was the administrative assistant at the State Department of Education under several state superintendents. He continues to serve the University of Mississippi in the same capacity. Dr. Mullins had the unique ability to recognize problems that existed in the administration and provided leadership for the people who he worked for. He authored a book on education reform during the William Winter administration and remains an advocate for progressive education in Mississippi.

MARY HILL
A long time food service director for JPS. A solid administrator and one of the best food service directors in the state, in my opinion.

JACK RICE
Jack was the assistant principal at Hardy and Siwell Junior High Schools when I was the principal of those schools. He was

instrumental in helping me to achieve our goals of educating our students. Jack was cooperative, and we made a good team. He later became an administrator in the Pearl School District until his retirement. Jack was fair-minded in every situation that came up at our schools.

CHUCK JORDAN

When I was a superintendent in Greenville, we hosted the grand marshal for the Rose Bowl in 1995. Chuck was then a banker in Greenville, and I needed some support to help lead a fund drive to assist students who could not pay their fare to the Rose Bowl. He was instrumental in organizing the community to raise $50,000 in a three-week period for the band to go to the Rose Bowl.

MARSHA MEEKS KELLY

Marsha Kelly served as the executive director of the Mississippi Volunteer Commission for many years, and she served in a very admirable way. She had the uncanny ability to keep others from saying no to her for volunteer causes. Ms. Marsha Barbour, the first lady at the time, was a standing member of this commission, and I learned so much about the work that this commission does from her as she served on the JMG board. I am positive that Ms. Marsha Barbour was instrumental in getting me appointed to the volunteer commission for two different stints, with the last stint served as the chairman of the commission. I learned so much about the value of the volunteer commission from Ms. Marsha Kelly that I feel obligated to mention the value of the program to the state of Mississippi. The members of the commission volunteer their time and are first responders to countless disasters whether they are hurricanes or tornados. In my opinion, the volunteer commission has the ability to fill the void for the need for volunteers at any time, and it is because of Kelly's personality and love for volunteerism that the program grew to be one of the best in the nation.

PART III

PHOTOS

Dorothy and Joe A. Haynes

Left to Right: Son, Christopher, Wife, Dorothy, Granddaughter, Erriona, Daughter, Kristi, Granddaughter, Kristion, and myself.

(Photo by J Johnson)

The check that my father, Allen Haynes, used to pay for 45 acres of land mentioned in the *Family* chapter.

College Board (IHL) 1990 with Commissioner Ray Cleere

Joe Haynes and Robert Wilson doing a writing session.
(Photo by E. Stone)

Donation to JMG from MySouth organization. *(Photo by JMG)*

Left to Right: Myself, Leisha Pickering, Kay Van Skiver, president of the JMG board (2007)

Joe Haynes and Athletic Director for Ole Miss, Warner
Alford

(Photo by W. Hickman)

Joe Haynes and former roommate from the University of Georgia, Eddie Stone.

(Photo by R. Wilson)

NFL Europe crew of officials in Barcelona, Spain
(Photo by S. Stenson)

NFL officiating crew

(Photo by J. Stewart)

Joe Haynes at football game in Philadelphia in 1986
(Photo by W. Thomas)

PART IV

OFFICIATING

CHAPTER ELEVEN

High School Officiating

In the fall of 1963, I was offered a coaching and teaching job at New Hymn High School by the late Mr. Lovell Gray. Mr. Gray knew of my wishes to become a teacher early on. He had promised me, when I first started college, that he would give me a job as a teacher. After becoming a teacher and basketball coach, I was able to convince Mr. Gray to let me start the first ever football team for New Hymn. Many of the young people on the team had never played football before, but the principal was able to go along with my desire to become a football coach and allowed me to form a team. Because it was a small school, many of the players on the new football team had originally only played basketball, and, now, they played both. However, the players were eager and able to juggle both sports. I am grateful for the opportunity to be involved in football coaching that led to my introduction to officiating.

Mr. Gray was such a generous and family-oriented person that he allowed my wife to teach at the school as a business education instructor, and he was instrumental in helping me further my high school officiating career, which led to officiating in junior college, senior college, and finally, the NFL. I am thankful for his support and encouragement.

I officiated my first game in 1964 in Columbia when Jim Hill came down to play. Jim Hill was from the big city of Jackson, and they had a band. My high school coach was the coach for Columbia. I was twenty-two years old. Lamar Lenior was the referee. They wanted a young guy, who was fairly competent, to help them officiate this game. They said, "Joe played football at Alcorn, so he ought to know a little bit."

I figured I could, at least, stand up and look like an official. During the game, I threw a flag—clipping below the waist—but I picked it up and gave it to the referee.

THE MOVE TO THE MHSAA

The schools were integrated in January of 1970, and all of the high schools were forced to join the Mississippi High School Activities Association (MHSAA). The black schools had previously been members of the Magnolia High School Activities Association.

We had a chance to officiate in the MHSAA, but the Magnolia officials got upset and called us bad names. They called us turncoats and Uncle Toms. But we saw the bigger picture. We had to lay the groundwork, and we were opening up doors. But we had to be good officials and had to have the temperament to deal with the issues that came along with that. There were some officials that wouldn't officiate with black officials, and we had to overcome those obstacles. The blacks were mad at us for taking our talents over there, and MHSAA's assigning secretary, Hank Bufkin, had some repercussions from some white officials about us being there to try to officiate with them. They said, "This is our game, and the blacks are taking money from us."

But it soon dissipated because the quality stood out. It was a chance for people to see that we could officiate.

"After they made the changeover, the schools couldn't use the officials from the Magnolia Association," Frank Bluntson said. "The coaches at those schools came to us and wanted us to officiate their games, so we needed to be a part of the MHSAA. At that time, the Magnolia Association had a lawsuit going on, and they wanted us to stick together and not go to the MHSAA. But about five or six of us guys said we weren't going to do that. These guys need officials they know, and we need to represent them because we had been calling their games for all these years. We went and talked to Hank Bufkin and told him that we wanted to join the MHSAA. Hank talked to us and said, "Okay, y'all can join."

Hank Bufkin was the assigning secretary of the MHSAA officials. Talmadge Portis, Joe Haynes, Jesse James, and Frank Bluntson were some of the first officials to join the MHSAA. We were calling the games in the second semester. The officials that stayed with the Magnolia didn't like the fact that we left. They said we were going to damage the lawsuit.

"They did a story about us in the newspaper. It was difficult because we were seen as traitors. We were forging new territory in a new officiating group. All we were doing was demonstrating that we could officiate with anybody, whether they were black or white athletes. I believe we did a great job."

"We got together the next summer and met at the police training academy," Bluntson said. "Magnolia had about twenty-five to thirty and the MHSAA had sixty-five to seventy. They elected the president and vice-president. One had to be black, and the other had to be white. Hank Bufkin was nominated. So, they needed to elect a black guy, and they had to work together. Joe Lyons nominated Frank Bluntson for assistant secretary. LT Smith stood up in the meeting and said, 'No. no. You can't do that. The law says one must be white and one must be black.' Lyons said to LT, 'What color is Frank Bluntson?' And LT said, 'That's not what I'm talking about.' They did vote me in, and we worked together for twenty years in football."

Hank brought in some ideas and thoughts. In baseball, he would always work the plate, and I would work the bases. He would correct me all the time. Hank was a rough dude. He would give blacks and whites alike a hard time. Hank was very opinionated and didn't mince words. To the average person, he might have appeared to be the crudest guy on the earth, but Hank was a good guy, deep down. I was in Greenville working as superintendent when Hank died, and I made sure I attended his funeral. That's how much I thought of him.

Hank used to call me late at night, especially during turkey season, because he used to hunt at Port Gibson, and he always wanted me to find umpires because there were some rainouts. My wife would say, "It's Hank," and I would know exactly what he wanted.

I was the assistant secretary. He would also call my office during the day to see if I could find someone to umpire at the last minute.

"My first football game was down 49 Highway in Magee. I was the referee, and I was the only black person on the crew," Frank Bluntson said. "It was the first time I have ever been nervous. All these highway patrols were at the game. You know a lot of the highway patrol officers came to these country games. They were lined all up and down the field. And I didn't see any black folks at all at the game. Nothing but white folks. I said to myself, 'Gosh, dog. They don't have any black folks around here.' We were out in the middle of the field, and we got the coin toss, and we were talking to the clock operator. We left to go to our positions. I will never forget. I was running down to my position, and I heard someone say, 'Hey, brother. Hey, brother.' I looked back, and there were about two hundred black folks in the corner of the field. No wonder I didn't see any black folks in the stands. One of the other officials, Tommy Bufkin, said, 'We will protect you tonight because we have to go to Lanier next week, and you've got to protect us.' The game went smoothly, and everything was fine. Before the game, I took about an hour to shine my shoes because I wanted to look like an NFL official for that game.

"We were blazing a trail for the future, and we had to do it right. We had to set the standard. We didn't want people saying we couldn't do it. I don't think anyone could've done a better job than Frank Bluntson. I knew the rules; I knew the mechanics. I knew I was a good official and was confident in my abilities and, also, in those of my fellow officials like Joe from the Magnolia Association."

THE QUICKEST GAME I EVER CALLED IN BASEBALL

There was ice hitting my windshield as I drove down to Florence for the game. It was early March, so it was pretty cold. I was the home plate umpire, and Frank Bluntson was working the bases. It was 1973. Hal Lusk was a left-handed pitcher from Florence. Stewart Cliburn was a right-handed pitcher from Forest Hill. Both were on. I mean on. They didn't miss. I told the hitters that they better get their bats off their shoulders because these guys were hitting the plate consistently. One of the Forest Hill boys hit a home run, and those were the only runs of the game. There were two balls hit out of the infield.

"I've been coaching for four decades, but I remember that game like it was yesterday," said Moose Perry, who was coaching Forest Hill then. "Stewart and Hal both had great games. Stewart had two good pitches, a good fastball, and a changeup that was effective because he changed speeds. Stewart struck out the first batter, but not the next four. There was a single, then Hal Lusk hit a ground-rule double to put runners on second and third with two outs. A player grounded out or flew out to end the inning. Stewart struck out the next eighteen batters. Stan, his twin brother, hit a two run homer in the top of the first inning, and we won 2-0. Hal was a crafty left-hander who was always around the plate and had a good curveball. Stan's home run might have been the only hit we had that day. Hal knew Stan and Stewart because they hung around each other a lot."

Stewart went on to play at Delta State and then was drafted in the third round of the major league draft. After a few years in the minors, he came in fifth in the voting for the American League Rookie of the Year with the California Angels. Then, he suffered a career-ending shoulder injury the next season. He went on to be a pitching coach. Stan was drafted in the fifth round out of high school and made it to the major leagues. He has been a minor league manager for many years and is now managing an independent team in Arizona.

"It is one of my favorite games in my high school career. I remember it like it was yesterday," said Hal Lusk, who went on to play at Belhaven College, coached at Central Hinds Academy in Raymond and at Brandon High, was the Jackson Public Schools athletic director and has been a Division I men's basketball official for twenty years. "We played on our old field by our old gym. We had no grass, all dirt. I think I struck out about fifteen batters, and Stewart struck out about eighteen. My dad and granddad were there, and they like to talk about that game."

CHAPTER TWELVE

High School Officiating and Charles Boston

I owe Charles Boston a lot. He helped make me into the man I am today. Not only did he help mold me into a good football player, he encouraged me to not turn away from an opportunity to play college football and, also, was the one who got me involved in officiating. Coach Boston was my mentor, my coach, and my friend. He was an exceptional teacher, excellent leader and coach, and a magnificent man. Coach Boston carried himself with dignity and respect and was able to gain respect from those around him. He was an inspirational leader and was able to create a way for people to contribute to making something extraordinary happen. Coach Boston made me feel like I was somebody.

First, I'd like to expound upon Coach Boston's involvement in my football career. Coach Boston was only my coach in my senior year at Bassfield, but he was a major influence in my life. If he had been my coach for all three years of high school, I honestly believe I would have been a pro-football player. He coached Walter Payton when he was coaching in Columbia. My senior year was Coach Boston's first year as a coach, but you would have never known it.

Bassfield was a little country town. Coach Boston brought uplifting ideas to a group of young people who were energetic but didn't know what to do. In other words, we played football, and we enjoyed it, but we didn't know what we were doing. We had a coach who didn't know how to do the schemes, so Charles Boston brought the know-how and the personality that was needed to win. He did more than just coach. He would take us hunting and that, in itself, made us interested in what he was doing.

As a coach, Coach Boston had to find the player. Because he came to my house and took me hunting, Coach Boston made me want to be in shape to play football the next year. He had shown interest that was unheard of in a country area. He would take Bill Graves and me to the movies and spend time with us to expose us. He had just finished college and had recently gotten married, but he would invite us over to his house.

Coach Boston taught us how to win. We had lost all of our games as juniors. The coach we had before Coach Boston had never played football before. We played a single wing, and I played tailback, but we couldn't score. I probably gained about one thousand yards each in my sophomore and junior years, but we couldn't get across the goal line. We did, however, with Coach Boston.

He would come out to practice with a sheet of paper with two plays on it. He would walk everyone through the plays. Coach Boston would put in two plays a day. The off tackle play was thirty-six. My number was thirty-six. The tackle and end were blocking on the play. It was almost a sure ten yards every time we ran it. It wasn't a job to learn the plays. That's where my philosophy of rules developed. Keep it simple. You can have more rules than you can enforce. Sometimes, we need to ask the question: "Why are we making this rule?" The less rules, the better chance you have of enforcing them.

One of my most vivid memories of my senior season was a play that I ran against Columbia. I will never forget it. We wore white pants that night. Green jerseys, gold numbers. It was 0-0 in the first half. I ran the thirty-six play, and I got outside, ran about forty yards down the sidelines, and got tackled at the goal line. And Boston came up to me and said, "Joe, you should have scored. You shouldn't ever get that close and let somebody tackle you."

And although that was fifty years ago, I still see it like it was yesterday. I can see myself going down the sideline and getting so close, but I didn't score. And we didn't score. He loved me enough to tell me that I didn't have the guts that I should have had at that goal line (I did not score when I was close to the goal line). He said that I was a big guy and that when I got to the three-yard line, no one should ever stop me from scoring. When I didn't score, it deflated the team.

"Joe was probably the biggest guy on the team, and I put him at fullback," said Boston, who coached at Bassfield for five years before going to Columbia for fifteen years. He had the fieldhouse at Columbia named after him. "Joe ran hard. You could hear him running. He had good feet, was a good-sized kid, and came from a good family. I remember that run because Joe made a really great run and had gotten close to the goal line, but he started strutting around because he was so proud of his run. I told him he should have taken that last guy and scored. Joe got the message."

Coach Boston also wanted us to get to the next level. He wanted me to play college football. I had an offer from two or three community colleges, but I didn't have one from Alcorn. That was my home school. My mother had graduated from Alcorn, and I wanted to go there. Dwight Fisher was at Wiley College in Texas, and he had been Boston's coach, and he offered me a scholarship because of Boston. Utica and Coahoma Junior Colleges offered me scholarships, as well. I was a good football player. I had potential, but I wasn't polished. I told Coach Boston that I wanted to go to Alcorn. Coach Boston told me he knew Coach Simmons at Alcorn. Coach Boston had played for him at Alcorn.

We went out there in mid-August. I was seventeen years old and 225 pounds. I had my foot locker in his trunk. We drove up to the athletic building. At that time, it was under the Oakland Memorial Auditorium. Under it was a deep basement. All the equipment was under there. Coach Simmons came out from under there with his whistle and his white T-shirt on.

He leaned over in the car and said, "What are you doing here? What position do you play?"

I said, "Fullback."

He said, "I don't need any more fullbacks."

Just like that. Man, I was seventeen years old, and tears started coming out of my eyes.

"Coach, let's just go back home," I said.

"No," Coach Boston said. "You get out there and get after it."

Practice, at that time, had ninety-five players, and they were only going to keep sixty-five. The grass was tall. It had not been cut intentionally. Jack Spinks and Marino Casem were the headhunters. They had us rolling around in the grass. If you weren't mighty good, you would go home anyway. We got out there for two-a-days, and it was hot. I worked hard.

My roommate was Ernest Reese. I told Ernest that I was going downstairs because Dr. Simmons said he was going to put up the list of the guys who made the team in the athletic dorm — Vet Dorm 2. I didn't want anyone to see me looking for my name, because, if I had gotten cut, it would be embarrassing.

He'd tacked it on the wall. I looked at the bottom of the list for 61-65. As I was looking, tears started streaming down my cheeks. I didn't make it! I looked at the top. My name was there. I remember what Coach Boston had said, "Get out there and get after it. Work hard at it and see what happens." I had made the team as a walk-on. I had surprised myself. The only reason I was able to make that team was because of the coaching and the support that Coach Boston had given. Not only did he help me to get there and encourage me to stay, but I made the team. To my amazement, Dr. Simmons said in the Alcorn football press guide about me that "I came to play, and I came to stay." Coach Boston kept up with me all during the time I was at Alcorn, and he also came to my games. He was keeping up with his product.

Coach Boston also helped me get my start in officiating. I was coaching football at Pinola in Simpson County, and he invited me to come be an official at one of their games in Columbia. I was twenty-two years old, and it was 1964. Columbia was hosting Jim Hill, from the city of Jackson, and they had a band. Everything went fairly well except for one time when I threw a flag for clipping below the waist, but I really wasn't sure. Lamar Lenore was the referee. I picked up the flag and waved it off. Leo Moore, who was a fan then, threatened me about a poor call that I made. He was standing near the sideline. Leo went on to become a longtime official.

"Joe did a fair job in his first game," Boston said. "He wanted to learn more and asked a lot of questions about it. He had a good knowledge of football and went on to have a good career as an official."

CHARLES BOSTON

Coach Boston was my mentor in high school, and he was an excellent teacher. What I remember most about Coach Boston was that he knew how to put different plays in for us to run at Bassfield. Coach Boston would come to practice with fifteen to twenty of us and put in plays by drawing the plays on a sheet of paper or clipboard, and there was never more than two to three plays per day. This methodology was good for us; in that, we had a lot of plays that were taught in increments. Thusly, we all knew the plays because we were never overwhelmed with a lot of plays to remember on a particular day. Also, Coach Boston understood his players "to the tee". He would mingle with his players on a daily basis, go hunting and fishing with the idea that his players would get closer to him. Finally, Coach Boston taught us how to win at Bassfield. He performed miracles for a country school, and, not long after that, he was sought by many schools to be a head coach. Coach Boston coached Walter Payton, arguably the best running back to play in the NFL, at Columbia High School. Coach Boston gave me my first chance to officiate a football game and was always a constant supporter even after my college days.

KEN TILLAGE

Ken Tillage was a football player at Alcorn and a fraternity brother. Tillage had the uncanny ability to draw people together and to get the best out of his players in high school and college. He continues to be a good communicator and problem solver to this day, and I admire him for all of the things that he has been able to do.

ERNEST REESE

Ernest Reese was my first college roommate. What I remember about him the most was that he had an athletic scholarship as a quarterback when he came to Alcorn, and I had a tryout for a scholarship. We would often talk about the chance of making the team as a walk-on and my concern, with so many players at the fullback position, that I would not make the team. He would always say that I must continue to work hard and that making the team would take care of itself. I remember his encouragement and our friendship. Ernest would later become a sports writer for the *Atlanta Journal Constitution*. When I first made it to the NFL, Ernest called me to do a story about my officiating, and we would often talk to each other on the phone as I traveled through Atlanta to officiate NFL games.

BUTCH JONES

Coach Butch Jones was a Jackson State graduate, but spent, for the most part, his entire coaching career at Alcorn. He is an example of true dedication to the coaching profession. Butch and I served on the church deacon board together, and for a long time, we rarely saw eye to eye on anything, but the more I

worked with Butch, the more I became one of his greatest
admirers and supporters. One thing was for sure, Butch Jones
would tell you what was on his mind and be through with it. I
admired that most in him. When Coach Jones was at Alcorn and
I was on the College Board (IHL), it was obvious that he had the
respect of the president of the college, Dr. Walter Washington,
and his fellow coaching mates because of his sternness and
honesty.

FRANK BLUNTSON
We have always been friends, and we have always had similar
backgrounds as far as officiating is concerned. We often talk of
our officiating days and how we were supportive of each other
as we helped to integrate the officiating in the central Mississippi area when it was not a popular thing to do. Frank Bluntson
has been a servant to the people for many years, and he
continues to be.

BILL PRYOR
Bill Pryor was an official in the high school association, and he
had a great association with other high school officials. Bill was
always the person that critiqued the officials in a crew, and he
was very instrumental in recommending me to his colleague,
Johnny Grace, who was an SEC official for many years. I am
sure that his critiques and evaluations with Johnny Grace
resulted in my first interview with him and other SEC officials.

BILL MOOSE PERRY
Coach Perry was an excellent baseball coach during my high
school umpiring days, and Coach Perry would support umpires
to the hilt. However, he would question certain things without

it becoming an issue with the umpires during the game. His players respected his demeanor. Coach Perry coached the Cliburn brothers that went on to play major league and professional baseball. His teams were always well coached, and they always played by the rules.

TYREE MCBETH

Coach McBeth was one of Jackson's best high school coaches in my opinion. I had a chance to work with him at Brinkley High School in the late sixties, and it was obvious that his players respected him and played for him. His demeanor was very easy and never demanding.

ORSMOND JORDON

Orsmond Jordon was one of the coaches that coached at a very high level until his retirement. Coach Jordon had the ability to get the best out of his players at all times. His record speaks for itself. He was a winner at all of the schools he coached, and he is a member of the Mississippi Coaches Hall of Fame because of his coaching and teaching in the Jackson Public School District.

JAMES BROOKS

James Brooks was the athletic director at Alcorn and an assistant football coach at Alcorn. I remember Coach Brooks and his know-how from my IHL days. I can recall many on point things that he did at Alcorn in order to make Alcorn a quality football team. James played a huge role in supporting Mr. Woodrow Marsh at the Mississippi High School Activities Association. His ability to recognize quality served the association well for many years.

WOODROW MARSH

Woodrow Marsh was the supervisor of the Mississippi High School Activities Association when I became the first minority to serve on the governing body in Kansas City. His honesty and fair play served the association in a respectful manner, in spite of the many issues that would arise at the high school association in those days. I served on the executive board and had firsthand knowledge of his involvement.

MIKE KENT

Mike Kent was the baseball coach at Madison Central High School when I was an umpire. He had the uncanny ability to make umpires angry without doing anything that would cause them to throw him out of the game. Coach Kent was extremely fiery but was able to control his emotions quite well in games. He knew how to motivate his players at the precise time to become winners in most games.

LEO MOORE

Leo Moore was a great high school official and served as a mentor to many high school officials and offered a lot of good advice to all officials, including me. For instance, at one game we were working together, I was, for lack of a better description, not giving it my all. Leo came to me quietly and gave me motivation to work harder and to give my best effort. He was always a motivational person and supported many causes that were on the right side of right.

BOB HILL

Bob Hill was the football coach at Jackson State at one time, and he had the ability to motivate his players. I had a chance to get Bob Hill to officiate some of my high school football games in the early days. We played at one o'clock on Friday, and he could get off to be an official and not many could do that at that time. He was a motivational person and believed in hard work.

HARRISON HAL

Harrison Hal was the basketball coach at Provine High School when I was the assistant principal. Coach Hal had the ability to manage energetic basketball players as well as anyone that I have ever seen; however, he also had the ability to get officials' attention by saying quiet insults without getting fans or players riled up. He could coach fast break basketball as well as anyone that I have officiated for over the years.

LAMAR LEINOR

Lamar was the official in the very first high school game that I ever officiated. His support of me as an official was superb. He allowed me to learn how to become a football official with him and Arthur Dampier as the senior officials. They would correct my mistakes and continue to work with me on my officiating techniques and mechanics.

D.M. HOWIE

Coach Howie was an excellent baseball coach at St. Joseph for years. I used to call many of his games as a baseball umpire. However, one game stands out more than any of the others.

Coach Howie and St. Joe were at Brandon High School at ten A.M. for a game, and I had the honor of working as the plate umpire. I called a strike on one of St. Joe's players, and Coach Howie came running down the first base line in protest. I called Coach Howie to the side and requested that he not do that again, and, if he did, I would throw him out of the game. Following the next pitch, he did the exact same thing, and I kept my promise. His players rallied behind this act, and St. Joe won the game. Later, I saw Coach Howie, and he explained to me that, had I not thrown him out, he did not feel that his players would have rallied to win. In other words, it was his intention to get thrown out of the game to wake his players up.

NATHANIAL ANDERSON
Nathanial Anderson and I were the two first minority officials in the SEC. We worked together for several years until I left the conference and went to the NFL. Nate and I were roommates during our training sessions and games together. Nate went on to work more than 25 years in the SEC and worked many major bowl games including the Rose Bowl game. Nate and I had a lot in common. We were both educators and we could relate to each other.

CLIFTON GRAVES JR.
Clifton Graves Jr. (Bill Joe) and I were classmates and Coach Boston used us as team leaders in 1959. Our senior season, when we had much success as winners, Bill played the split-end position and was also an excellent blocker from the end position. Bill Joe went on to become the elementary principal of our former high school, Carver High.

CHAPTER THIRTEEN

Junior College Officiating

A s I was moving up the ladder as a high school official, I had some interesting opportunities. One of those opportunities was to become the first black junior college official. I had worked at some high school playoff games and a bowl game or two, and the call came in the form of an invitation to join the Mississippi Junior College Officials Association. I served on Captain Bill Grisset's junior college crew. This opportunity provided me with college experience at the junior college level. After joining Grisset's crew, I soon found that officiating in the junior college ranks had its privileges and requirements. Grisset drove us to most of the games in his van; however, all officials had responsibilities on each game date. We usually officiated junior college games on Thursday nights during the season with a rare Saturday night game. Our responsibility as crew members was to be responsible for the food and beverages that we would have after the game and on our return trip to Jackson. We had some interesting opportunities and conversations riding in the seven passenger van.

I can recall one game in which Grisset did not referee the game. Buddy Oliver was the referee in a game that we had in Northeast Mississippi, Columbus. We had an uneventful game; however, on our drive back to Jackson, by way of the Natchez Trace as we neared the Ridgeland Exit, we noticed that a park ranger was pulling us over. We might have been speeding because we had such a great conversation going on that was entertaining to the driver, as well as entertaining to the officials in the car. I was sitting in the back seat, and I took it upon myself to get out and speak with the ranger, and he told me to get back in the car and shut my mouth. He, then, proceeded to write Buddy Oliver a ticket for speeding on the Natchez Trace. That episode taught me many things.

The junior college experience was valuable to me as I moved to the SEC, and later, to the NFL. I learned about crew work and some of the ins and outs of being in a crew. I thank Bill Grisset for asking me to join the junior college ranks back then when the pay for each official (5) was thirty-five dollars per game. During my stint with the Junior College Officiating Association, I had a chance to work NCAA college football, mainly Millsaps College. The good part about officiating NCAA football at the small college level was that it allowed me to come into contact with Coach Harper Davis, the head coach at Millsaps College. Coach Davis was a great football player at Mississippi State and a hall of famer. It was obvious that he and his assistant, Tommy Raneger, were on top of the coaching situation at Millsaps College because they were the only two coaches with whom we had to deal. I am grateful to the many officials that I have worked with in the junior college ranks: Bill Grisset, Buddy Oliver, Hansel King, Hank Buffkin, O.H. Simmons, George Harden, Demery Grubbs, Harold Cooper, Marvin Hogan and many others that I had the opportunity to work with.

CHAPTER FOURTEEN

Major College Officiating

(Getting into the SEC)

I was one of the first two black officials in the Southeastern Conference. It was an interesting journey.

It started when Butch Lambert Sr., one of the top officials in the SEC, came to a meeting at our Magnolia High School Association, the association over the black schools in Mississippi. This was back in the 1970s. There was a lot of racial tension at the time. It was during the time of integration, and Butch and others in the SEC wanted to integrate the officiating crew.

Butch Lambert was different. He was a humanitarian. A diplomat. I remember this day like yesterday. He had on a pin-striped sports coat. I can see him standing up there right now, and that was forty plus years ago. He was sent at the right time to make a difference. He didn't upset anybody.

Johnny Grace came to my office at Jackson Provine High School out of the clear blue. I was an assistant principal, at the time, at Provine. I didn't know Johnny Grace from Adam's house cat. Johnny wore glasses and had a terse voice.

"Joe, I want to talk to you," he said.

He sat down, and we talked.

"We're getting ready to integrate the SEC, and we need some black officials."

Alabama coach, Bear Bryant, and Auburn coach, Shug
Jordan, were among the coaches on the coaches' committee.
During that time, if you didn't have the support of the coaches,
you could forget it. They controlled the officials, in my opinion.
There had to be some good guys out there somewhere they
thought. Johnny Grace had his right hand man (Bill Pryor)
working in his office. He was an umpire. He also worked at
State Farm. He had told Johnny Grace that he thought I'd make
a good official. He wasn't that interested in my officiating as
much as he was my humanitarianism and my ability to get
along with people. Johnny went to one of my games on Friday
night and watched me officiate. He said he didn't find me
running anybody down. He had nothing but good things to say
about me. I'm sure that he told Cliff Harper because Johnny
wanted me to apply for the SEC.

The SEC supervisor of officials, Cliff Harper, and the dean of
SEC officials, Pete Williams, who was also, the head referee for
that Saturday's game, met with me, and we stayed at the Sun N'
Sand hotel in downtown Jackson the Friday before an SEC
game. They wanted to come down and talk to me and see what
a guy who thinks he is going to be an SEC official looks like.
Remember now, this was two weeks into the season. Pete went
to the Naval Academy. I talked to Pete and Cliff and some more
officials. They gave me the once over, and that was it. I think I
went to the game. It was the 1973 season. I got an application
and I applied. I didn't get in until 1974. They submitted my
application in 1973, and I was rejected.

During Auburn's spring practice in 1973, some black players
didn't go to practice one day. They boycotted, and that infuriat-
ed Shug Jordan. He didn't want people to think those guys had

caused him to change his attitude. He decided to delay any black officials from getting into the SEC. That is unwritten. Butch Lambert Sr. told me this story years later. I'm not here to try to dig up any bones. There are two ways to get where you want to be. There is the wrong way, and there is the right way.

Once I got into the SEC, Palmer Manning did a story in the *Clarion-Ledger*. People called me and said, "There are ten or twelve officials that are better than you!" Instead of congratulating me, they were upset at me. The first impression I had was to get upset because people were being jealous or angry. But I didn't take that attitude. I wrote every official in the association and thanked them for helping me to get into the SEC. My secretary, Jan Mercer, did it for me. This achievement could have been anyone, but it was me. And I went into this, too, in the letter. The SEC's goal was to expand. I understand there was some jealousy. What they didn't understand was that this was paving the way for them to come later. After I wrote that letter, it calmed the doubters.

AUBURN COACH PAT DYE

I was working a game between Auburn and Kentucky at Commonwealth Stadium in Lexington, KY. Bo Jackson — one of the best running backs in the history of the SEC — ran a sweep to the left side and ran out of bounds, very close to the first down marker. I was the line judge on that side, the Auburn sidelines, and Auburn head coach, Pat Dye, came running down the sidelines to where I was. I had put my foot where Bo had gone out of bounds, and it was just a few inches shy of the first down. Coach Dye put his foot right beside mine, but his foot was on the other side of the first down marker. In other words, Coach

Dye's foot showed that Bo had made the first down. My mark showed that he had barely fallen short of it.

I told Coach Dye, "No, no, coach. He ran out right here, not there."

Coach Dye put up a fight and fussed and talked about it for a while.

Before every football season, we found out what games we had to officiate for that season. To my surprise, I had four games with Auburn. And Gorden Pettus, the SEC supervisor of officials, told me that I was the only official to get four games with Auburn. Four is the maximum number we were allowed for each team each season. Gorden told me that Coach Dye said he liked me as an official because, "Whatever he said it was, that's what it was going to be." I stood by my calls. It verified that I was on the right track with my officiating.

"Joe was one of the greatest officials in the SEC," Coach Dye said. "That's the reason why he made the NFL because he was one of the top ones in our conference. Joe was consistent and good. The best officials are the ones who you don't know they are out there, and the games run smoothly. Joe was absolutely one of those.

"We were playing a critical game, and Bo made a run that I thought was a first down. I would try to influence an official if I could and would make no qualms about it. Joe marked the ball short of the first down and let me know real quick that was it, and he wasn't going to change it. He stood his ground no matter what I did or said. Now, that's a great official. Joe was one of those who didn't care who was on the sidelines or what they said. He wasn't going to change the call, and I admired him for that."

MY COLLISION WITH HERSCHEL WALKER

One of the most famous photos of college football was when Georgia's Heisman Trophy winner, Herschel Walker, stretched out parallel near the goal line and jumped, it seemed, ten yards for a touchdown against Ole Miss during the 1981 season at Oxford. Walker ran all over the Rebels that day, gaining 265 yards on an amazing forty-one carries. He looked and ran like Superman.

I remember that game for a much different reason. I was the clock operator for that game. Sometime during that game, Herschel came around the end, and someone knocked him out of bounds, and he hit me. He knocked me flat on my behind. I jumped right up. You've got to remember how big and strong Herschel was. He was 6'1" tall and 225 pounds, pure muscle. Remember the *Sports Illustrated* story about him doing thousands of pushups every day? I felt the result of all those pushups. Steve Sloan, Ole Miss' head coach, ran down to see if I was okay. Man, I was hurting all over, but my youthful pride wouldn't let me tell Coach Sloan that I was hurting. If it was now, I would have stayed down. I told Coach Sloan that I was fine, but I was about to faint. For the next five minutes, I could have dropped. That's how weak I felt. Coach Sloan knew I was hurting. Anyone who was hit by Herschel, even with pads on, felt it, and I didn't have pads on. That was probably the hardest hit I've ever taken as an official.

BUTCH LAMBERT SR.

Butch Lambert Sr. had just retired and was the supervisor of officials for the SEC. He came to the Florida-Auburn game in Gainesville that weekend. Butch Lambert Jr., myself, and some more officials were at the game. We were sitting there like a bunch of turkeys, about to get cut. Butch Lambert Sr. said we seemed to be uptight. We didn't have much experience among any of us, and they carried us in a van to the game with a motorcycle escort. The game was going to be televised on ABC. Butch wanted to calm us down, and he told this story. He was working the Florida State-Florida game. Butch was a line judge, and he had this guy on the other end of the line. There were about 85,000 people there, screaming and hollering. They were down on the goal line, and it was third down. The player plunged the line. The guy on the other side of the field came running in with his hand halfway up. Butch said to himself, "Oh, gosh. What is going to happen? Are we going to get off the field safely?"

After that game, he always prayed to the Good Lord, "If there is ever going to be a close play, let it be on my side of the field, so I can make the call." He told that story, and it helped relax us and was a reminder to be confident in our abilities. I remember that to this day because it is another example of giving me confidence. You can't be hoping for someone else to make that call, you've got to want to make that call. It is like a quarterback wanting to have the ball on the last drive of the game because he has the confidence to win it. You have to have that mindset.

MY LAST SEC GAME

My last college game as an official was an intense game between Alabama and LSU in noisy Tiger Stadium in November of 1983. There were about 90,000 screaming fans. If you have ever been to Tiger Stadium, you know what I mean. It is so loud that you can hardly hear yourself talk. It is one of the greatest places to watch a college football game. But it can be incredibly difficult for an official, especially when he makes a call against the home Tigers.

Late in the game, an Alabama player picked up a loose ball and ran for a touchdown. I wasn't sure if I should have called the ball dead or not, so I bought some time by running onto the field. It gave me some time to think about it. I was still going out there and something told me not to blow. I had a finger on the whistle. I looked across the field and saw that he'd gotten the ball clean. All of this happened in a few seconds. I had to make a split-second decision, and I decided not to blow the whistle. I'm glad I didn't. There is no telling what would have happened if I had blown the whistle. If I had blown the whistle, the NFL would have definitely heard about it in my opinion. I may have never gotten an opportunity to be an NFL official. I'm serious. The NFL doesn't like negative publicity. There's no telling what would have happened. I mean, it was a big, big game, and that was a big, big play. There were fanatics on both sides. If I had made the wrong call, it would have been talked about all across the television and across the nation. The NFL might have just said, "Let's stay away from this guy. We don't need to take someone who is going to blow a call like that in a big game. He might do the same thing when he calls one of our games." It would have hurt me. Thank goodness I didn't throw the flag too soon.

CHAPTER FIFTEEN

NFL Officiating

(The Road to the NFL)

I had applied to the NFL early in my career as an SEC official, but I found out that I needed more experience to become an NFL official. Once I had the experience, I applied again. This was in 1982. Nick Scorch, a former coach for the Philadelphia Eagles, came to Jackson and interviewed me to be an NFL official. I felt good about the interview, and a few weeks later, I was notified by letter that I'd had a good interview, but I didn't make it. The letter said, if I was still interested, to apply again. "Write us and we will schedule you to be interviewed next year."

Several months later, I got a call from Jack Reader, who was over NFL officials recruiting at that time, and he wanted my schedule for officiating in the SEC in 1983. I sent it in and realized they were interested.

I was working a game at Auburn, and I noticed this guy behind me on the sidelines. Every time I looked back, he was there. He had a long coat and hat on, and I couldn't figure out who he was. I remember thinking, Who is this dude? The tight end moved and came back and got set. That was legal. The quarterback waited until the tight end got set before he snapped the ball. I didn't throw my flag. The guy behind me said, "You're right."

At that point, I thought, Maybe I am being observed.

About February 1984, Nick Scorch called me and asked me if I was sitting down. I told him no. He said, "Well, sit down and welcome to the NFL."

I was an incredibly happy guy. Several papers wrote stories about me making it to the NFL. I was on a high; I was in the newspaper, and I got a lot of letters congratulating me on making it to the NFL.

BOBBY BOYLSTON PUT THE IDEA IN MY HEAD

Bobby Boylston was an SEC official from 1966-77 and an NFL official on the field from 1978-98. He retired because of his knees, and he is now an instant replay official. He lives in Duluth, Georgia. Bobby was also a sporting goods equipment salesman, and he called me one time while he was traveling through Mississippi. We had become friends in the SEC.

"I asked him why he doesn't apply to be an NFL official," Boylson said. "Joe said he had never really thought about it. Well, doggone it! He got in. And it's not easy to get into the NFL as an official. There are probably 500 to 1,000 people who apply every year. It's really tough. You have to be interviewed, scouted, and take sports psychology tests. There's a ton of scrutiny on you.

"But Joe is a good man, a good official, and very conscientious. I've always been impressed with him. He did a good job in the SEC and NFL. He doesn't carry a chip on his shoulder. Joe got along with everybody. He is a quiet guy, a great person, does a lot of charity work. I've always been impressed with his attitude. There weren't many black officials in the NFL then, but Joe mixed well with everyone. Joe would call me for advice. He was always trying to learn and seek information. Joe has overcome a lot of obstacles. He is respected by many."

MY FIRST IMPRESSION OF ART MCNALLY

In my first year of being an SEC official, I thought I would apply to be an NFL official and see what happened. I applied and didn't know if I would ever hear back, but to my surprise, I received a very nice letter from the NFL supervisor of officials, Art McNally. He not only thanked me for applying to become an NFL official, but explained to me what I needed to do to become one. He could just have said, "No, you aren't qualified" and left it at that, but he took the time to write me a personal letter. There is no telling how many letters like that he got a week, but he took the time to write me, and that made a huge impression on me and showed me what type of man and leader he is.

ART MCNALLY IS A GREAT LEADER

Art McNally is a great human being. He is, in my opinion, the consummate leader. He is a guy you can talk to. Art is a master with his leadership skills. He was not a pushover. Art understood his role. He was competent. Art had been an NBA official, a college football and basketball official, and an NFL referee. He had been a teacher. Art knew how to get along with people. He had high performance standards, and he conveyed his confidence to his people.

While he helped me gain confidence, Art didn't sugarcoat anything. If you didn't know what you were doing, he told it like it was, but he permitted you to have an opinion. Most of the time, you solved your own problem. If you let people talk about it, they will eventually see your side, and that's what Art did. It doesn't work when you just tell them to shut up and not talk, that won't work. Art encouraged participation. All of the NFL officials were not the same when we arrived, in terms of talent, and Art recognized that. We all came to the table with a different set of tools and had different strengths and different weaknesses. If you can't recognize that in a leadership position, you aren't going to be able to do a good job. You could have a diamond in the rough and not know it. Like former Oklahoma Coach Barry Switzer had with Marcus Dupree. Coach Switzer said that he didn't handle Marcus Dupree right, and he recognized that after it happened. He said that's the worst mistake he made coaching. That's where having the special touch like Art McNally comes in. He was an effective manager. He listened, he encouraged, he planned, and he was approachable.

THE PEACHES STORY

Art did something in his hometown that made a huge impression on me. I know it is a small thing, and most people may not think much about it, but it showed how Art was, how he understood people. We were in Philadelphia, PA. Art had always been pretty healthy and had two peaches in his carry bag. Fred Wyatt, our referee, knew how to get under Art's skin. Fred took one of the peaches and ate it. Now, Art had one peach left. Art knew I wanted a piece, so he gave me half. That went a long way with me as to how he dealt with adverse situations. In other words, he could see I wanted a piece, and he didn't get on to Fred for taking one. He demonstrated that he had the ability to see my desire to have the peach.

MY FIRST GAME

In my very first preseason game in the NFL, Art McNally knew I was dying. He was at the game between the Washington Redskins and the New England Patriots at JFK Stadium. This was a televised preseason game. Art was our supervisor that night. Pat Summerall and John Madden were doing the game for CBS. The game was tape delayed.

While I was down on the goal line, I saw this big gaping hole. I was the line judge, so I went up with a half signal for a touchdown, but I was unsure. This linebacker came from somewhere and knocked this guy off the line; the ball went up in the air. It was a fumble, and I wasn't sure whether it was a touchdown or not. I made a half touchdown signal. The point I'm trying to make is Art, being the supervisor of officials, knew I was feeling bad in the car going back to the hotel after the game.

Art said, "Joe, did you call a touchdown?"

I said, "Yes."

Art said, "Was it a touchdown?"

I said, "I really don't know."

Art said, "You've got to figure that out. If you are going to work in the NFL, you are going to have to know if it was a touchdown or not."

Art knew I had done this. What he respected me for was that I didn't deny it. I accepted the fact that I had made a mistake.

Art said, "Here's what I want you to do. If you are going to work in the NFL, you are going to have to be sure there was a score when you make that call. I want you to go to your hotel room and watch the replay of the game."

So, here I was watching it at two in the morning. The game got to where I made that call, and John Madden said, "Didn't that official on this side give a touchdown signal?"

As I was sitting there, my heart jumped out of my chest. I learned a lot from that. I learned two things. It was a preseason game, so it didn't hurt anybody, but Art McNally basically told me that I could do better than that and that I was going to have to do better than that. But he did it in a great fashion. In other words, he said I'd made a mistake, but I could do better. He came to me with the redemption and the idea that I was going to be all right. I needed to not worry about it and instead, learn from it. It was something I was going to have to work on. All through my career, I have thought of things like that. It was my first preseason game, and I had to come to grips with that. I never made that mistake again.

THE FIRST BLACK MAN IN THE WHITE HAT

I was on Fred Wyatt's crew, and we were officiating a game between the New England Patriots and Baltimore Colts in Boston. It turned out to be a historic game for me. I was the line judge when our referee in the crew, Fred Wyatt, was injured in the third quarter. Fred asked me to replace him. This action made me the first black person to wear the referee's white hat.

"Joe was in all the headlines of all the black magazines for being the first black referee in the NFL. He became a celebrity," Fred Wyatt said. "We kidded each other all the time. I'd always tell that him, if he would let me lead the Alcorn A&M band at halftime and also walk the nicest looking black girl down the street in Jackson, I would make him the first black referee in the NFL. We had a great time, and I was glad he made history that day.

"We were on a kickoff, and I came in to spot the ball. A player came in late and landed on my shin and sprained my ankle. I couldn't walk, so I took off my white hat and told Joe, 'Here. Now, you are the first black official.' His eyes got really wide. 'You go back in there, and, on the kickoff, hold up your hand, indicate when ready, and give the signal.' He was there for one play, and then I took back over.

"The NFL put Joe on my crew because they knew I would help him relax. I would leave my crew alone and let them do their jobs," Fred said. "We would work twenty weekends a year. I wouldn't trade it for anything. We had a great time, and Joe had a great time. I would kid with Joe to help him relax. We were there for him. We were serious about our work, but we also had a good time. Joe was warm, caring, attentive, and intelligent. He had a PhD. Maybe three to five out of 110 officials in the NFL had PhDs then. He was a smart guy, and I really enjoyed his company."

THE SETUP BY AL DAVIS

The Oakland Raiders were playing host to the Cincinnati Bengals at the Los Angeles Coliseum in September, 1984. I was in my first year of being an NFL official.

I would always walk out onto the field early and check it out to make sure that everything was in place.

Someone walked up behind me and started talking. It was the Raiders owner, Al Davis.

"Hey, Joe," Al said. "How's Walter Payton doing? How's (former Jackson State football coach) W.C. (Gorden) doing?"

I started talking to Al. Then, he started talking about all of these landmarks in Jackson. Stuff that only people who lived in Jackson would know. Dick Hantak told me that I needed to leave Al alone. He said Al was trying to set me up, in other words, soften me up, so I would give the Raiders a break during the game.

I was the line judge on the Raiders' sideline. Al walked that sideline. My job was to key on the offensive right tackle and make sure he didn't do anything illegal. Al kept hollering about the Cincinnati right tackle holding. I finally threw a flag on the tackle for holding and Fred Wyatt, our referee, administrated the ten-yard penalty. Dick was the back judge and came up to me and said, "Joe, that wasn't holding. This guy had his arm up, and the guy tried to run through it. He didn't hold him. Joe, that's a bad call. You aren't going to get a good grade for that. What happened here was that Al kept working on you until you threw the flag."

Al Davis was setting me up. I guaranteed myself then that I would probably get a bad grade for that, and I did. Everybody on the Bengals was upset at me. I mean, here was Anthony Munoz, an NFL All-Pro offensive tackle, and this rookie line judge was throwing a flag for something Anthony had legally been doing for years.

RAYMOND BERRY'S CLASS ACT

I was the line judge for a televised game between the Miami Dolphins and New England Patriots in 1984. New England went on to play in the Super Bowl that year.

I had made a call that looked like it might determine who won the game. This was before instant replay, so whatever the official said stood. I called offensive holding on a play when the Patriots scored a touchdown. The fans — 85,000 of them — weren't happy. Raymond Berry, the Patriots' head coach, was standing right behind me. I stood there with the flag on the ground, and my heart was beating fast. I was hoping the call was right. Raymond Berry got on his headset and talked to his assistant coaches upstairs. Although there wasn't instant replay then, the coaches had access to see the play again. Raymond walked up to me and told me that his assistants said it was a good call. The players were very upset, calling me all kinds of names. After telling me that it was a good call, Raymond turned around and told his players to stop hollering at me.

I got a chance to thank Raymond years later. He was a guest speaker at the Jackson Touchdown Club on November 16, 2009. The Touchdown Club gets together every Monday during the football season to talk about various games and recognize outstanding performances. There is a different speaker each week. After the speaker finishes his message, there is a time for questions. I am a member, and I attend every week I can. I definitely made it this Monday night. After Raymond finished his talk, I spoke up.

"I don't have a question, but I have a comment to make," I said before I retold the story. "Coach, you might remember and you might not. I was a young official in the NFL, and I had thrown a flag for holding on your right tackle. You can't believe how relieved I was when you told me it was a good call. It means more to me now than it did then. Little things like that make a difference."

The people in the audience were very appreciative of him. We don't give credit to people for a lot of good things that they do, and I wanted to recognize him for doing that for me.

NO HARM, NO FOUL

Legendary coach Bud Grant came out of retirement to rejoin the Minnesota Vikings. My fellow officials had always told me that Bud wasn't one to say much during a game. Fred Wyatt, the head of my officiating crew, said Bud was a quiet spirit. So, when I was assigned a Vikings game with Bud as the coach for the first time in my officiating career, I didn't think there was going to be any problems on his sideline. Boy, was I wrong.

A linebacker came in with a forearm and barely missed hitting the running back in the back of the head. If he had hit him, he would have been paralyzed. I threw a flag, and Bud went ballistic. Dick Hantak was the back judge and asked me if the player hit the running back. I told Dick that he didn't. Dick said, "Don't call that then."

I quoted the rule book. There is a rule that covers flagrant activity. A penalty is to be assessed if one player deliberately attempts to strike another player illegally. In this case, that did not happen. It's a judgement thing. Dick knew I knew the rule book. It was the letter of the law, but not necessarily the best common sense.

Art McNally said, "Joe, I tell you what. I'm going to give you credit for the call, but don't ever do it again as long as you are in the NFL."

In other words, no harm, no foul. That's the purpose behind it. That's judgement.

WORKING AS AN UMPIRE IN TOKYO

I got the opportunity to work the World Bowl game between the Houston Oilers and the Dallas Cowboys in Tokyo, Japan, in 1990. It was a great experience. The Japanese fans would cheer whenever everyone else cheered because they didn't know much at all about the game of football. I was in my normal position as one of the line judges, but in the middle of the third quarter, the umpire got hurt and could not continue to work his position. In fact, they sent him back to the United States before the game was over. We had said before the game that, if one of the officials got hurt, I would be the first person to take that position because we could do without the line judge. So, in I went into the middle of the field as the umpire. I realized it was a tough position. I had people step on my ankles. I was so sore. I didn't want to look like a rookie, but it was a difficult position to be in on the field. The NFL supervisor of officials said I looked like a veteran umpire. I think they were being extremely kind. I didn't think I did a very good job out there. I hoped I didn't do too good a job because I would much rather be a line judge than an umpire. It was a good experience, but thankfully, I didn't have to make that switch in my position again.

BETTER GET IT RIGHT

Rod Woodson is one of the greatest defensive backs in the history of the NFL. A 2009 NFL Hall of Fame inductee, Woodson has more interception return yards than any player in NFL history.

I was the line judge for a Pittsburgh Steelers game one year. Woodson was playing cornerback on my side. And he got beat.

That didn't happen very often. The receiver caught the ball and ran for a touchdown. Woodson wasn't happy. And that was an understatement. Woodson grabbed the pylon at the corner of the end zone and threw it into the stands. Here came my flag. *BOOM!*

The league office didn't like a whole lot of flags. "If you can't prove it, don't mess with it" was their motto. The next week, I got my score back, and they had a question mark by that particular flag. It was a fifteen yard penalty for unsportsmanlike conduct administered on the kickoff. NFL supervisor of officials, Art McNally, called me and said, "Joe, what did he do?"

I said, "He picked up the pylon and threw it up in the stands."

They liked to see that on film for support. I had to hope that they didn't get a call on Monday from the owners because they wanted to support me with the film. The owners own the league. They want to make sure the officials aren't getting harassed by the owners. They went two weeks, and they finally found the film. I thought they had forgotten it. Someone had it where the young man took the pylon and threw it into the stands. They didn't give me a good grade until they saw it. That was the way they operated. I could understand that. If they couldn't see it, they called it a phantom call. The worse thing that could happen to you was that you throw your flag and it was not there. There are many times I wish I had it back before it hit the ground. The bottom line is this — as an official, you only throw your penalty marker when you are sure a foul has occurred.

JOE THEISMANN

I was on the field for one of the most gruesome scenes in the history of the NFL.

It was a Monday night game between the Giants and the Redskins at RFK Stadium in Washington, D.C.

Dave Moss spotted the ball in the middle of the field. He called me Mississippi. He was the game umpire.

Giants linebacker, Lawrence Taylor, one of the best defensive players to ever play the game, hit Redskins quarterback, Joe Theismann. He came around, got past his offensive tackle and tackled Theismann. I was the line judge on the Redskins sidelines. Lawrence Taylor was calling medics to the field. We called timeout. We went over and saw that his leg was disfigured. It was hard to look at. It was the worst injury I have ever seen. I couldn't look at it because I was trying to figure out how agonizing that must be for that quarterback. That game changed my whole attitude about players. In a quick minute, they cannot be able to play again. Get it while you can because you never know when it will be over. That's why Brett Favre's streak was so remarkable. He was out there a long time.

Joe Thiesmann's injury was replayed on the movie *The Blind Side*, the popular story about former Ole Miss offensive tackle, Michael Oher. It is one of the opening scenes because it talks about how important an offensive tackle is in the game of football. I was referee No. 112. You can see my back in the movie.

DO YOUR JOB

I learned not to listen to coaches and to just do my job in 1987 during the strike season.

Let me set the scene: The New Orleans Saints played the Philadelphia Eagles in Veterans Stadium in Philadelphia. Because of the strike, both teams played with replacement players. Also, because of the strike, the fans had put a human ring around the stadium. But our supervisor knew this was going to happen, so he called us the day before. He wanted us to get to the stadium early in the morning before the fans got there. The whole idea was for no one to cross the picket line. So officials didn't get caught up in all of this, we got there early, went to the stadium club house, slept on the floor, and ate there.

Eagles head coach, Buddy Ryan, wanted to get the game over quickly. He raised sand every time we threw a flag and would yell out, "What are you slowing down the game for?"

So, I decided I wouldn't throw my flag anymore. The Saints had a split end and would not line up correctly, but I didn't throw the flag much. I missed being an official in a playoff game because I got so many bad grades in that game. I went back, did my math, and checked it. That's the game that cost me. I was trying to get the game over, but it didn't work out.

Buddy Ryan was making such a fuss that I thought I would accommodate him, but I shouldn't have. The NFL supervisor of the officials then, Nick Scorch, graded the film and gave me some bad grades. He told me that I had to make those calls. He said that I had a job to do and to let the coaches do theirs. The game never would have gotten over, but maybe I would have called a playoff game that year if I had made those calls.

*****

When I was officiating in the NFL, I had a chance to meet Coach Eddie Khayat. At that time, he was an assistant coach with the Boston Patriots. During a timeout, I had a chance to introduce myself to him, and he and I related to each other extremely well because of his brother, Chancellor Khayat, who, at that time, worked for the University of Mississippi as dean of the law school, and later, as the chancellor of the university. During the time that Eddie Khayat was a coach in the NFL, we talked about Mississippi and his hometown of Moss Point, Mississippi on equal footing.

*****

When I was a new official in the NFL, Art McNally, the director of officials, was instrumental in getting Bob Beeks to mentor me since Bob Beeks worked the line judge position to perfection, and that was also my position as an official. Beeks was incredibly effective in helping me to gain confidence as a new line judge in the NFL. I later learned that I was working with one of the best line judges to ever officiate in the NFL. According to McNally, he seldom made a mistake. He is one of five officials that worked the Super Bowl five different times, which, in itself, is a feat. Beeks worked in the NFL for twenty-two years and was a policeman in St. Louis while working in the NFL.

CHAPTER SIXTEEN

Mentoring in the NFL

(Coaches, Officials, and Players)

T he following players are those who played in the National Football League and who made an impact on me during my officiating days in the league. Twenty years later, they stand out in my mind above all the rest of the thousands of players in the games where I was an official. Not necessarily because of how talented they were, but more so because of how they carried themselves or how they had a positive influence on their teammates, coaches, and opponents and were good role models for kids and adults to follow.

BEN WILLIAMS (former star at Ole Miss from Yazoo City, Mississippi and an All-Pro defensive end with the Buffalo Bills from 1976-1985)

I was working a game at Buffalo, and I was the line judge on the Buffalo sidelines. Marv Levy was the coach for the Bills, and there was some controversy about a call, and I was getting criticized because of a call on the field. Ben was standing there on the sidelines, and I knew Ben from working scrimmages when he played at Ole Miss. I walked up to Ben and I said, "Your teammates are giving me hell. You need to get on them."

Ben said, "I am on this team, and I understand where you are, but I can't do that."

Ben was honest with me, and later, during a timeout, we talked about it. I made a mistake by asking him to do that. I wanted Ben to say, "Hey! Shut up, guys. I know this man, and he is from my hometown."

But Ben couldn't because of his relationship with his teammates. He couldn't be my savior. In other words, he couldn't step forward and keep his teammates from getting on me. And from that day forward, Ben and I have had some great conversations about that time in our lives and how I learned from that.

WALTER PAYTON (Columbia, Mississippi native and Jackson State star who was a two-time NFL MVP and an NFL Hall of Fame selection with the Chicago Bears from 1975-1987.)

I've known Walter since his days at Jackson State. He did his student teaching in special education at Provine when I was an assistant principal there. He has always been friendly, but the NFL doesn't like players to fraternize with the officials during the games, so he did it another way.

I was working a game at Soldier Field in Chicago. It was early in the fall and an unusually warm day in Chicago. Walter shot around the end where I was working as a line judge, and there was a big pile up. All of a sudden, I felt something on my calf, like a bunch of bumblebees were stinging me. As my calf tightened up, I realized it was Walter. He was under the pile, but he had reached out and was squeezing my leg. It was his way of speaking to me.

Although Walter is known as possibly the greatest running back in NFL history, he is also known for his compassion for kids. Our officiating crew always had a Christmas party for underprivileged kids, and we were in New Jersey one year. I found out Walter was going to be in the area, and he volunteered his time to come talk to the kids at a hotel. We would also get some companies to give clothes or shoes, and we needed a celebrity speaker to talk to the kids. The kids were on top of the world because, not only did they receive great Christmas gifts, they got a chance to meet and talk with one of the best players in NFL history. They and I will never forget it. That's the kind of guy Walter Payton was.

ARCHIE MANNING (Drew, Mississippi native and former Ole Miss star quarterback who played for the New Orleans Saints from 1971-1982, Houston Oilers from 1982-83 and Minnesota Vikings from 1983-84. Archie is the father of NFL quarterbacks, Peyton and Eli Manning.)

At the end of his career, Archie played with the Vikings. He was standing on the sidelines of a game that I was officiating. I was the line judge on the Vikings sideline. I had never had a chance to talk to Archie much although I had admired him for years. Unfortunately, once quarterbacks in the NFL gets up in years, they become expendable, and they ship them off to another team to the end of their career. The Saints did that with Archie. I just couldn't visualize Archie Manning being on the sidelines. So, during a timeout, I went over and talked to him. He was very personable. He was the most humble guy you would ever want to meet. I was reluctant to ask him why he was standing on the sidelines and wanted to tell him that he should be playing. But, for Archie Manning, who had had a great career with the New Orleans Saints, to be a part of this team and contribute in many ways other than playing, stuck out in my mind as someone who was willing to help others improve. Archie was always like that. It wasn't about him.

Later on, Archie did a radio show, and I listened to him all the time. Archie was a balanced guy. I later had a chance to visit Archie's son, Eli, in Atlanta when he played at Ole Miss. Eli was just as humble and kind as his father. I wasn't in the league when Archie was getting pounded with the Saints, but I was there when he was at the end of his career, and I will never forget Archie's humbleness and unselfish attitude to help his teammates even when he wasn't playing.

KENT HULL (Greenwood, Mississippi native, who played center at Mississippi State and played for the Buffalo Bills from 1986-1996. Hull was the starting center in four Super Bowls. An example of his leadership was when he received the Ralph C. Wilson, Jr., Distinguished Service Award in 2001 by the Bills).

In my opinion, Kent Hull was the team leader of the Buffalo Bills. He was everything you would want in a player. He was extremely quiet, but he played hard every play. Kent didn't take off a play. He was full speed every play, every game, every season. I loved officiating a game that Kent played in. Kent was one of those guys that you took notice of. Kent was dominating. He played with a lot of character. Kent was a gentle giant. He exemplified leadership.

HERSCHEL WALKER (1982 Heisman Trophy winner from the University of Georgia who played for the Dallas Cowboys, Minnesota Vikings, Philadelphia Eagles and New York Giants from 1986-1997).

Herschel was playing for the Minnesota Vikings, and I was coming back from Minnesota. My flight was through Dallas, and Herschel and I were sitting in first class in the same row. I talked to him about the days at the University of Georgia and about how he ran over me at a game when he played against Ole Miss and I was the clock operator on the sideline. I told him that I was the deputy superintendent of Jackson Public Schools and that I tried to get people to come in and talk to kids. Those inner city kids needed to hear from someone who had made it. Herschel knew what I was talking about. I asked him to come to Jackson and speak, and he said he would love to and gave me his personal phone number. I couldn't believe it because I knew he was an incredibly busy guy. It never worked out for him to come to Jackson, but I will always remember how interested he was and how thoughtful he was about helping me and those inner city kids. Herschel overcame a lot during his pro football career, and I'm sure he has influenced thousands of youth along the way.

JOE MONTANA (Hall of Fame quarterback and two-time NFL Player of the Year who played for the San Francisco 49ers and Kansas City Chiefs from 1970-1994).

I was working a 1989 NFL Divisional playoff game between the San Francisco 49ers and the Minnesota Vikings at San Francisco. The 49ers wore them out (jumping out to a 27-3 halftime lead and cruising to a 41-13 victory). I'd always heard about Joe Montana, but hadn't been around him much at all until that game. Joe was a small guy with little legs, but he was an incredible quarterback. He rolled out to my side, and I thought he was going to be killed, but he threw a touchdown pass (one of four touchdown passes that day). I always liked to compliment guys when they do something good, so I walked up to him and told him that his throw was fantastic. He just smiled. I said to myself, "This can't be Joe Montana?"

You think these superstars have a cocky attitude, but many don't. Joe's attitude and demeanor were so humble. He had every right to be cocky. Joe was in the prime of his career and went on that season to win his fourth Super Bowl. Some experts say that the 49ers team that season was the best in NFL history. And Joe is recognized as one of the best quarterbacks in NFL history. But his smile, after the compliment, told me about his inner confidence and his outer humbleness.

JERRY RICE (Considered by many the best NFL player in history. The former Mississippi Valley State alumnus holds numerous NFL receiving records, including touchdowns and receptions. Rice played for the San Francisco 49ers, Oakland Raiders and Seattle Seahawks from 1985-2004).

I was the line judge for a 49ers home game at Candlestick Park. Joe Montana completed a long touchdown pass, but it had to come back because I threw a flag on Jerry. He went into motion too soon. I didn't know if he knew I was from Mississippi or not, but during a timeout, I mentioned to him that the best game I had ever seen in Mississippi Veterans Memorial Stadium in Jackson was between his team, Mississippi Valley, and Alcorn

State, where I played. I was off from officiating that weekend and was able to go to that game. There were 64,000 people, and it was standing room only. It was not only the best game I had seen in Jackson, but it was the best football game I had watched in my life. Jerry was reserved and didn't say anything, but he did say, "Mr. Official, what did I do wrong?"

I said, "You jumped early. False start."

In the mid-1980s, you continued to play (since then, they've changed the rule to stop play immediately), but we called it back.

Several years later, when I was the superintendent at Greenville, I got Jerry to autograph some footballs and used them to improve attendance in our schools. I gave away six or seven footballs during the year with Jerry's autograph to kids with perfect attendance. I wanted Jerry to autograph some more footballs, and his father-in-law got Jerry to autograph some more footballs at a golf tournament. Despite his success on the football field, Jerry has always been approachable and helpful to me. I appreciate and admire Jerry Rice for his incredible work ethic and commitment to being the best football player he could be. He did that his entire career, and it paid off in outstanding dividends.

BRETT FAVRE (The former Southern Miss quarterback is the only player in NFL history to win MVP three consecutive years, 1995-97. Favre played for the Atlanta Falcons, Green Bay Packers, New York Jets and Minnesota Vikings from 1991-2010. He holds the NFL record with 297 consecutive starts).

Brett Favre is known as one of the greatest quarterbacks in NFL history and became an NFL Hall of Famer with the Green Bay

Packers. But many might have forgotten Brett started his NFL
career with the Atlanta Falcons. I used to call a lot of Southern
Miss games when Brett was playing, and then I was a line judge
in the NFL when Brett was with Atlanta. I had a game in
Atlanta during Brett's rookie season with the Falcons. He was
on the sidelines and not playing. The Falcons were almost
forced to take him and took him in the second round of the 1991
NFL Draft. I was taken aback that he wasn't out there on the
field. I just spoke to him and told him I was surprised he was
not on the field. I can see him now, standing on the sideline in
that Atlanta Falcons jersey. The Falcons traded him to the
Packers before the next season for a first-round draft pick. The
rest is history. Brett went on to an incredible career with the
Packers.

STEVE MCNAIR (The NFL co-MVP in 2003, the Alcorn State
alumnus played quarterback for the Houston Oilers, Tennessee
Oilers, Tennessee Titans and Baltimore Ravens from 1995-2007.
McNair, from Mount Olive, was named the Division I-AA
Player of the Year while at Alcorn).

When I was on the State College Board, I got a chance to see
Steve McNair up close and personal during his great career at
Alcorn State. It was one of those times when Alcorn was down
by a lot, and Steve brought them back for a victory. I was the
guest of Alcorn's president, Walter Washington. I got a chance
to talk to Steve after the game, and he was a very humble guy.
His mother raised a great son. Even though I didn't get an
opportunity to officiate any of Steve's games in the NFL, I kept
up with him through the league and friends from Alcorn. He
continued to be a humble person despite his success. A lot of

credit goes to his mother, who was always extremely supportive of Steve and was always at his games at Alcorn.

RAYMOND BERRY

Raymond Berry was involved in one of the biggest highlights of sportsmanship in my NFL officiating career. I made an offensive holding call against the New England Patriots, and the 85,000 Patriots fans, the coaches, and players weren't happy with me. But Berry, the head coach, told me it was a good call and told his players to calm down.

Twenty-five years later, at a Jackson Touchdown Club meeting in Jackson, I got a chance to thank him when he was the key speaker. I told him how relieved I was when he told me it was a good call. It means more to me now than it did then. Little things like that make a difference. We don't give credit to people for a lot of good things that they do, and I wanted to recognize him for doing that for me.

BILL PARCELLS

Because of the Mississippi connections with coaches on his staff, Bill always had something nice to say or he would say something funny.

He couldn't help but get your mind off of the game. I don't care how good of an official you are, when you go out on the field, you get butterflies. If you don't, there is something wrong with you. Bill would walk up to me during the warm up time and say something funny and would give me the impression that he supported me. Remember, this was my early days in officiating, and it felt good to get support from someone like him. Bill was always warm.

MARTY SCHOTTENHEIMER

Marty was coaching for the Cleveland Browns during the mid-80s, and they were playing the Green Bay Packers in a preseason game in Milwaukee County Stadium. I was one of the line judges in the game. The Packers would play a certain number of games in Milwaukee. The unique thing about the game was that both benches were on the same side because of the way the baseball stadium was configured. There was a play that happened on my side of the field when Scottenheimer was close to it. He came to my rescue. He could tell I had a blank stare and didn't know what had happened. I had never seen it before. I think the ball went out of bounds. He came up to me and showed me where the ball should be placed. I remember that it was an act of sportsmanship. I was disappointed when he got fired. He wasn't just a good coach; he was a good person. You can tell a good person by the way they communicate with the officials on the sidelines, and Marty was one of the best and nicest coaches in the NFL.

NICK SKORICH

Nick came to Jackson to interview me for the NFL in 1983. We met in a hotel by the Jackson airport. Nick was a pipe smoker. He was about 5'8", a short, round guy from Philadelphia, Pennsylvania. He ended up being my best supporter. He told me that I was kind of thick and that I needed to trim down a little bit. That stood out in my mind. The next time he came back to Jackson, I was in better shape. I was in a better position to make the calls. I didn't get the appointment to the NFL my first year, but I did my second. Nick was always my go-to person. If something happened in a game and I wanted to know about it, I would call Nick. He would tell me the nuts and bolts about it. He was my friend in the league office.

During the season of the NFL players' strike, Nick called us at about two A.M. on a Sunday morning before a game in Philadelphia. We were at the Marriott by the airport. He told us to go to Franklin Field really early, way before the fans started showing up. Philadelphia was a blue collar town. Nick didn't want us to cross the picket line. We slept on the concrete to the sports club in the stadium. He didn't want people to say that Nick would break the picket lines in his hometown.

(They interviewed about fifteen people for the NFL in 1983, and Nick called me to tell me I didn't make it). In 1984, he called me and asked me if I was sitting down, and I was. He advised me, "Welcome to the NFL!"

Nick was an extremely good, no frills supervisor. If you did a good job, he would tell you. If you didn't, he would tell you.)

BOB WAGNER

What I remember most about Bob is that he would take the opportunity to have prayer and have a way to relieve ourselves of the pressures of officiating in a big ball game. We would pray and have testimonies. We would go to a vacant room or meeting room at the hotel. He would arrange it. He is a great guy. He is a college professor. The first time we met was at Oklahoma and Kentucky game when Philadelphia, Mississippi, native Marcus Dupree played for Oklahoma, at Commonwealth Stadium in Lexington. Bob was an official in the Big Eight, and I was in the SEC. We reunited in the NFL. I always remember that he was a pleasant person. (He would plan for a meeting room for our devotions, and it was powerful. Bob has always been a very good friend).

DICK HANTAK

I was on his crew for two years. He was also encouraging, but the thing about Dick was when I talked to Oakland Raiders owner, Al Davis, during my rookie season as an NFL official. Dick said, "Leave him alone because he is trying to get something."

I can see Dick now down the field just as soon as I called that foul on Raiders offensive lineman, Anthony Munoz. They didn't want that called.

Dick said, "I told you. That was not an NFL holding call, maybe in college, but not in the NFL. That was a poor call."

Dick was extremely helpful when he became a referee and I was on his crew. Dick was a good rules person, and he would recognize anything you were not doing and tell you.

BOB BOYLSTON

Bob has always been a supporter of mine. He was in Jackson selling sporting goods, and I met him at a sporting goods store on Ellis Avenue in South Jackson. He had just left the SEC and was headed to the NFL. I asked him how did he go to the NFL? He told me the steps to take. He went home and sent me an address, and that was the beginning of my road to the NFL. Bob was a friend all the way through my time in the SEC. I can't say that for everyone in the SEC. There were a couple of years when I was really struggling, and Bob knew it. He was the president of the association. Bob would always offer advice. He helped me get through the tough times and I'm very thankful for that.

LARRY UPSON (former director of officiating in NFL)

I learned a lot from Larry. After five years on the field as an NFL official, Larry became the director of officiating. He was an administrator. It is different than being an official. You've got to grade people; you've got to pick people for the playoffs; you've got to do things. He told me that some things he did, people didn't like. He had to make judgment calls, be subjective, and take votes from three or four supervisors. They were always talking about who should make it and who shouldn't. Larry told me that it was very tough to make these decisions. I could relate to that.

When I was in Jackson Public Schools, I had to do the same thing—having to lay off people, fire people and make decisions. So, I was fully aware of what Larry was up against and some of the pressures he was under. Larry taught me a lot about being a manager, being in charge of people and how to treat people. I believe I helped him, too. He spent the night with me in Jackson once, and we went to Hattiesburg together to watch an official at the Southern Miss game that might be good enough to be in the NFL one day. Larry was the kind of person that you could talk more than just football with. He was a level headed person and that explained why he was able to become the director of officiating in the NFL and later in the USFL.

DAVE PERRY (an NFL official for eleven years and supervisor of officials in the Big 10 until 2011)

In addition to being an NFL official for a decade, Dave was named the supervisor of officials for the World League. He had to make the decision about who was going to make the playoffs. He called me and said I had been selected to be the line judge in the first playoff game between Barcelona and New York in the European League. He told me he had been watching me, and I was the best official in the line judge group. I didn't know he was paying attention, but he was. I will always remember him for that. I didn't know him, but he was always pretty up front.

(Before the first championship game in New York City, Dave came to me and said, 'You are the best line judge we have on the field and you are going to be selected to work the playoff game,' the equivalent of the NFL championship game. I was surprised, and I had no idea he had been watching me so closely. Dave gave credit when credit was due.)

JOHNNY PARKER (former Assistant Coach at Ole Miss)

Bill Parcells always had something nice to say to me, and I'm sure that Johnny Parker, who was the strength coach with the Giants then had something to do with Coach Parcells knowing who I was and where I was from because of his association with Ole Miss. Johnny was extremely nice to me, and we would always talk on the sidelines. (Johnny was from the Delta originally, and he had a great personality.)

RED CASHION

Red was a referee in the NFL. Red and I used to work a lot together with the Saints because he was stationed in Texas. A lot of times the Saints would have scrimmages, and they would want NFL officials, and it was easy for us to get down to New Orleans. I got to know Red very well. He was a good official. He was noted for "first down", and he had a unique way of giving the first down signal on the radio or television. He was also a great official. He was a humanitarian, and I remember a lot of things Red taught me about being an official in the NFL.

FRITZ GRAF

His number (thirty-four) was retired after several years of use by Gerald Austin because he used his number. In the early days of replay, the Cowboys' Emmitt Smith caught a swing pass and ran about 5-to-8 yards, and the ball never stopped moving. I ruled it a fumble. Fritz looked at it in the replay, and he agreed. We both got graded down for a bad replay review. We got written up in the Dallas newspapers big time for something that even an instant replay couldn't determine.

JOHNNY SCHLEYER

Johnny and I worked on several crews together. John worked as the head linesman, and I worked as the line judge. During the season, many times, we had to have a working knowledge of how the head linesman was going to work, and John and I would communicate before a game on how we would call certain things if there was a question about them and how we would reserve our signals until we were on the same page.

DAVE ANDERSON

Dave was a line judge with me. He had a unique way of making good plays. Dave would make sure that we worked together similar to John Schleyer.

BILL COROLLO

Bill is now the supervisor of Big Ten officials. We worked on the same crew for several years in the NFL. His whole demeanor is extremely smooth. Bill could recognize if you were uptight about a call and tell you to forget it. Bill was the kind of guy who would give you encouragement and make sure you would not mess up the next play. He was a back judge and many times they could see things that you could not see as a line judge.

BOB RICE

I remember Bob Rice as an official and as a supervisor. The year that I worked the championship game between the Minnesota Vikings and the San Francisco 49ers, Bob Rice had been my supervisor. He graded my game films. He gained a lot of confidence in my skill. I respect Bob because he was very objective. I recall I had twelve major calls in the game and not a bad call during the game. That signified that he was objective and fair in grading the call.

ART MCNALLY

If you polled all of the officials, I imagine Art would be labeled as the favorite of all of the supervisors of officials in the history of the NFL. Art was the kind of guy you could talk to, but yet, he wouldn't take any gruff. He was an awfully good guy to talk to.

LEO MILES

Leo was an official in the NFL, and after he retired, he was the person in the NFL responsible for assigning scouts to work games. Leo would always give me a Monday morning report. After I sent in my report he would always call me and review it over the phone. He had a very good feel for the officials and what they had to endure. He was trained under Art McNally. I admired Leo because even though I had written a positive report, he wanted to hear a verbal report, too.

BURLE TOLER

Burle Toler was the first black official in the NFL. I didn't get a chance to work much with Burle, but I got a chance to meet him. He was a member of the San Francisco Dons basketball team. Burle was a great guy. Pete Rozelle was instrumental in him getting into the NFL. I got a chance to meet Burle when I went to the Western Clinics in the NFL and he was working in the west.

FRANK GLOVER

Frank was an NFL official and he was also in education. We were fraternity brothers and had some of the same issues on education. He lives in Atlanta and is a great friend.

TIMMY MILLIS

Tim was an NFL official, originally from Simpson County. He went to Millsaps and helped JMG for several years while he was executive director of the NFL retired officials association. I have a lot of respect for Tim because he was a humanitarian.

JOHNNY GREIR

Johnny Greir is currently a supervisor of officials for the NFL. What I liked about Johnny was that we had a chance to go to camp several times when I was an official. Johnny was the first full-time black referee. He was always consistent and knew the rules. Johnny did an excellent job as a referee and is a good human being.

NATE JONES

While Nate and I didn't work any games together because he was in the Western Conference, Nate and I had similar jobs. Nate used to be an assistant principal at a high school. He and I would relate to being NFL officials and educators.

TED COTTRELL

Ted was an assistant coach with the Buffalo Bills. In 1984, Ted and I walked off the field together. The NFL had a concern about fraternizing with the players and coaches. I received a call from the NFL office about walking with the coach. There was no harm done, but I was reminded that I needed to stay away from the coaches. We developed a friendship from that.

BEN MONTGOMERY

Ben was a line judge when I went to the NFL and he was one of the minority officials in the league. I had a chance to really talk to Ben about some of the issues associated with the rules and mechanics in the NFL. He was a guy you could always talk to. Ben was a fun guy to be around.

JAMES WILSON

James was an SEC official when I was in the NFL. I got to know James because he was a district manager for Ford trucks. He would come to my office after he got into the NFL and talk about some of the issues in the NFL. I told him to join the crowd because it was a tough job. After every game, it starts over again. James and I had good conversations about NFL officiating.

JACK VAUGHN

Jack was from Ponchatoula, Louisiana. He was an SEC and NFL official. He was probably a better NFL official than he was an SEC official. While I didn't work a lot with Jack, I got to know him pretty well. He stayed on the campus at Mississippi State. He had a son that went to Mississippi State. Jack and I worked a spring game at Mississippi State while we were both in the NFL. It was a special time because we got to support our alma mater. Jack and I discussed rules in the NFL a lot and he was a big help to me.

CHAPTER SEVENTEEN

Recruiting

(Scouting for New Officials for the NFL)

A fter I retired from officiating from the NFL in 1992, NFL commissioner Paul Tagliabue appointed me as an NFL scout. I also helped find officials for various conferences around the country for the NCAA. I'm always looking for good officials when I go to high school or college games. The NFL has about seventy scouts, and they all work together to find the best talent in the nation. I found Sarah Thomas that way.

Thomas was going to give up officiating and it was going to be her last game when I saw her.

"It was December 13, 2006, and I was an official in the Class 4A state championship game between Wayne County and Clarksdale," Thomas said. "It was going to be my last game. I had already told my husband that was going to be my last season and this was going to be my last game. But Joe saw me and thought I did a great job. He called me and we met soon after that. Joe asked me why I had not pursued my career further because he recognized that night that I was a good official. When I got into officiating, I just did it more out of curiosity with my brother and then I realized that this could be a challenge. I guess because of my competitive spirit it intrigued me to pursue it. But after ten years of officiating high school, I had decided to quit to spend more time with my boys, Bradley and Brady, and my husband, Brian.

"But because of Joe Haynes, I got plugged into doing college games through (Conference USA coordinator of game officials) Gerald Austin. I don't know where I would have been if Joe hadn't seen me at the championship game and showed enough interest to contact me. Instrumental is a word that I can't stress enough when it comes to Joe. He understands what it takes as an official to get there. Joe has a good eye for officials and relays it to young officials in a way they can understand. He is very encouraging.

"Joe called Gerald because they had worked on a crew together in the NFL. Joe told Gerald that there was an official that he needed to look at. Gerald said, 'What is his name?' Joe said, 'HER name is Sarah Thomas.' Joe and I met soon after at Jason's Deli in Northeast Jackson, and Joe told me I had what it took to be at the next level. I had no idea. He noticed my field presence, the way I looked in a uniform, my confidence on the field, things like that. When he said that, I didn't realize that would be what an NFL scout looked for. It was kind of a shock to me that they took all that into consideration.

"So, after we talked and Joe talked to Gerald, I worked a Southern Miss scrimmage where there were some officials who were plugged into Conference USA and then I worked a camp in Reno. That's where Gerald hired me."

Sarah became the first female to officiate a Division I football game. She has done well. In fact, she graded out as the best at her position (line judge) and earned a spot in the Conference USA championship game in 2010. She also has worked in the United Football League and did so well she officiated in the championship game in her first season.

Walt Anderson was the head referee in the 2011 Super Bowl. I saw him for the first time several years ago and told my supervisor Leo Miles about him. Walt was the best official in the game and I relayed that information to Leo. They sent him a letter and asked Walt to apply. He became an NFL official and now he has reached the highest level — the head referee in the Super Bowl. Walt has worked two Super Bowls, four championship games and been in the playoffs in each of his fifteen seasons. He is one of the best officials in the NFL. He has been a referee since 2003.

"Joe discovered me at a Southland Conference game at Natchitoches, La., at Northwestern State in 1990 or 1991," Anderson said. "Joe had come to watch a couple of other guys who possibly could be NFL officials, but I caught Joe's eye. When the NFL asked Joe about the game, he said those guys were OK, but there's a kid named Walt Anderson who they needed to look at. Joe asked if they had a file on me and they said they had never heard of me. I sent in my application and five years later, I was in the NFL. I had never expressed interest in the NFL because I thought my next step would be the Southwest Conference. After Joe told the NFL about me, the league contacted Banks Williams, who was an official in the NFL at that time and knew me because he was from the Houston area. He called me and I remember I told him that was a surprise because I had never thought about going to the NFL.

"I was very humbled and honored to work the Super Bowl. The first time I worked the Super Bowl was Super Bowl 35 in 2000 and I was a line judge. Calling a Super Bowl game was a lot of fun. It was a good game and a great venue. I am very thankful Joe saw me that night."

Chris Cockrell was working at a high school game at Pisgah and I noticed him. And now Chris is an experienced Division I and Arena League official.

"Dr. Haynes has a good eye for talent and is fair and honest and he tells you about your work and critiques you," said Cockrell, who has been officiating in the SWAC and Arena League for seven years, Conference USA for five years and United Football League for two years. "Dr. Haynes has really helped me a lot with my officiating career and has been a good mentor for me. He has helped me with my on the field mechanics and helped me learn how to handle things. Dr. Haynes is a great ambassador to the officiating profession. He is always encouraging and always tells me to stick it out. Any time I have a question, all I have to do is call Dr. Haynes and he is there to give me good answers and sound advice. He has a lot of wisdom and knowledge about officiating."

I helped Yazoo City native, Herbert Owens, get into the Southeastern Conference.

"Dr. Haynes is a great official and a better person. If it hadn't been for black officials like Dr. Haynes breaking the barriers long ago, guys like me wouldn't have had the opportunities we do today," said Owens, who has been an official in several conferences before getting into the SEC. "Dr. Haynes gives great advice on on-the-field expectations of officials. He keeps you motivated and helps you to want to work hard and learn. He keeps you grounded, focused and responsible. Dr. Haynes has taught me to be respectful on and off the field with everyone you run into contact with. He has a great knowledge of the game and the rules and mechanics of officiating and is so good with younger officials at clinics."

~About the Author~

Dr. Joe A. Haynes, former Superintendent of Greenville Public School District, has worked with numerous school districts and universities in Mississippi, including Holmes County School District, Jackson Public Schools, and Jackson State University. Dr. Haynes served as the Associated Superintendent of Leadership and Operations at the Mississippi State Department of Education. He is the former Executive Director at Jobs for Mississippi Graduates, Inc.

Dr. Haynes also has a long history of working with the National Football League as an Official – Line Judge, and he continues as an NFL College and University Talent Scout for Prospective NFL Game Officials. He is a member of the National Alliance Black School Educators (NASBE), American Association of School Administrators (AASA), Mississippi Association of School Administrators (MASA), and Association for Supervision and Curriculum Development (ASCD).

Dr. Haynes is available for radio, print and television interviews. If you are interested in scheduling an interview, appearance or book signing, please contact publicist Shonna Pierce by phone at (601) 410-1974, or by email at shonnakaypierce@aol.com.

To learn more about upcoming events for Dr. Haynes, please visit his website at www.drjoehaynes.com

~Bio for Robert Wilson~

Robert Wilson is a national award-winning sportswriter, author, teacher, tutor, publisher and mentor from Jackson, Mississippi. Wilson won dozens of awards on the national, state and local levels in his 23 years as a sportswriter for *The Clarion-Ledger*, Mississippi's largest newspaper, and has written stories for national publications. He is well known among Mississippians for his ability to paint a picture of the subject he is writing about and not only about their ability, but about their personality as well. Wilson also has the reputation of taking students who aren't performing very well and some in at-risk situations and turning their lives and grades around with one-on-one sessions. He is the co-author of *Don't Throw the Flag Too Soon*, a memoir of Dr. Joe Haynes, who is a former executive director of Jobs for Mississippi Graduates.